English Translation: Robert Allen

Living Architecture:
CHINESE

MICHÈLE PIRAZZOLI-T'SERSTEVENS

Keeper of the Musée Guimet

Research by Nicholas Bouvier, assisted by Denise Blum

Macdonald · London

Editor of Series   Henri Stierlin
Plans   José L. Conesa

SBN   356 03853 X
             Printed in Switzerland

Photo-composition   Filmsatz AG, Berne
Printing Text and Plans Buri Druck, Berne
Heliogravure plates   Roto-Sadag S.A., Geneva
Offset reproductions   Aberegg-Steiner & Cie S.A., Berne
Binding   Buchbinderei Burkhardt, Zurich

© Office du Livre   Published in Great Britain in 1972 by
Fribourg 1971   Macdonald & Co. (Publishers) Ltd.,
                         St Giles House, 49/50 Poland Street, London W.1.

Contents

Foreword

No aspect of Chinese culture has been more neglected than architecture. This is due largely to the erroneous reports of western travellers during the eighteenth and nineteenth centuries. Even Sir William Chambers visited only Canton and judged all Chinese architecture by what he saw there. His works, which enjoyed a large readership during the second half of the eighteenth century, helped to spread in Europe the idea of an architecture at once monotonous and uninspired and of an art of gardening viewed through western eyes and judged by western conventions.

When more objective studies were undertaken at the end of the nineteenth century, they were hampered by problems linked with the very essence of Chinese architecture. The impermanence of timber structures and the imprecision of the texts in which they were described seemed almost insuperable obstacles. As a matter of fact, the works of the Chinese and Japanese archaeologists showed that this impermanence was only relative. Indeed thirty or more edifices built between the eleventh century and the thirteenth are still extant and count among the oldest timber structures in the world. Moreover, the fragility of the material is made up for by a remarkable preservation of types and forms.

The problems are complex, nonetheless. Successive reconstructions and restorations have modified the original aspect of a great many ancient monuments and make it difficult to study architectural evolution; a great many documents have not yet been collated; the terminology is often rather vague and lacks equivalents in western languages. But the immense strides made by Sinology in the last fifty years, the many diggings, and a better knowledge of the country, its cultural constants and the phases of its history will throw new, more searching light on Chinese architecture and town planning.

Incidentally, many aspects of this art bring it close to contemporary western views.

This little book could not have been written were it not for the works of the eminent scholars who first studied the subject and solved the most arduous problems it raised. Let me acknowledge my indebtedness in particular to Professor Paul Demiéville, Professor Alexander Soper and the late Professor Osvald Sirén.

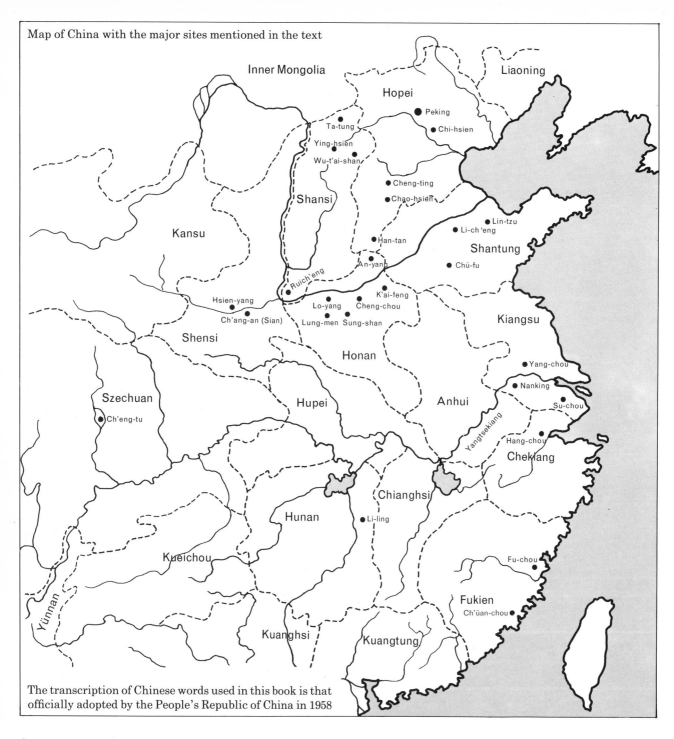

Map of China with the major sites mentioned in the text

Inner Mongolia

Liaoning

Hopei

Peking
Ta-tung
Chi-hsien
Ying-hsien
Wu-t'ai-shan
Shansi
Cheng-ting
Chao-hsien
Kansu
Lin-tzu
Li-ch'eng
Han-tan
Shantung
An-yang
Chü-fu
Ruich'eng
K'ai-feng
Hsien-yang
Lo-yang
Cheng-chou
Kiangsu
Ch'ang-an (Sian)
Lung-men
Sung-shan
Shensi
Honan
Yang-chou
Szechuan
Hupei
Anhui
Nanking
Su-chou
Ch'eng-tu
Yangtsekiang
Hang-chou
Chekiang
Chianghsi
Hunan
Li-ling
Kueichou
Fu-chou
Yünnan
Fukien
Kuanghsi
Ch'üan-chou
Kuangtung

The transcription of Chinese words used in this book is that
officially adopted by the People's Republic of China in 1958

4

1. The Cultural Context

The time has not yet come to study the regional aspects of Chinese art. But that vast country, equal in area to the whole of Europe, offers contrasts in climate, orography and population that have left their mark on all its artistic creations. Suffice it here to insist on the most obvious and drastic of these contrasts – that between the north and the south.

Northern China is a land of vast plains and plateaux, of wheat, millet, gaoliang and soya, where the climate is mostly cold and dry, travel easy, the villages built of clay, and the towns laid out on a chessboard plan with wide streets and low houses.

The south, in contrast, is a jumble of hills and dales, where travel is difficult and rainfall copious. It is a country of rice, cotton and tea, and of towns with narrow paved streets overshadowed by many-storeyed houses.

This disparity is matched by a complex human geography that cannot be concealed by the preponderance of the Han race (the people traditionally called Chinese) and the apparent unity this entails. For Chinese culture has constantly evolved in contact with the non-Chinese peoples that were attracted towards its frontiers. As these peoples became part of the community, they were gradually assimilated to the Han after contributing to the civilization that absorbed them certain customs, ideas and expressions of their own.

Chinese civilization was long reproached with immobilism by Occidentals who were disappointed at not finding there anything resembling the European conditions they were accustomed to. In its historical evolution that civilization gives the impression of being precariously balanced between a traditional, unchanging vision of the world and periodical upheavals that brought progress, innovation and discovery. Chinese society, which was dominated for 2,000 years by a ruling class of literate officials, is fundamentally agrarian. Built up of autarkic peasant cells sparsely scattered over an immense territory, it would have collapsed into anarchy had it not been for the solid framework set up by the administrators sent out by the central government. Side by side with this stabilizing factor, the existence and rivalry of several national states on Chinese soil led periodically to a relapse into feudalism or the rise of a merchant middle class whose development was always hampered by the government machine as soon as the unity of the country was once again consolidated.

Ancient China

After a neolothic period that was extremely rich in Northern China, the first use of bronze and script was accompanied along the middle reaches of the Yellow River by the rise of the first historical dynasty, the Shang (seventeenth to ninth centuries B.C.). While a semi-sedentary peasantry engaged in animal husbandry and tillage based on temporary land clearance, the nobility spent their time hunting, fighting and attending religious ceremonies presided over by the king. Religion seems at that time to have been a complex assortment of cosmological concepts, myths, divinatory practices and beliefs dominated by ancestor worship and the cult of the Sun, which symbolized the nurturing soil and the deified domain. This civilization, which occupied only a very small portion of the Chinese territory, produced fortified towns and buildings erected on terraced earthworks, as is demonstrated in the traces of two Shang capitals discovered at Zhenzhou and Anyang in Henan.

In 1028 B.C. the Shang dynasty, weakened by incessant struggles against non-Chinese populations, was ousted by the Zhou, who came from the western province of Shânxi. Once they had occupied the ancient domain of the Shang, the Zhou granted fiefs to allied clans.

During the eighth century B.C. advances in land clearance and husbandry incited the major vassals to extend their domains and seek hegemony. The wars they waged from the eighth century to the sixth produced the first political structures and a certain organization of relations between the various states. This development took place behind the economic and religious screen of an enfeebled Zhou dynasty whose last refuge was a small territory in Henan.

It was speeded up in the fifth century by the invention of cast iron (documented from 513 B.C.) and of the harnessed plough. New techniques led to better tools and promoted the use of permanent irrigation.

Output rose, population increased, new lands were colonized to the west and south. The principalities united to form great states whose struggles gave their name to the epoch of the Warring States that lasted from the fifth to the third century B.C.

The expansion of the principalities brought with it the formation of new economic circuits, an expansion of the Chinese cultural area, and exchanges between different nations in the Chinese world.

The emancipation of the artisan class fostered a mercantile spirit that gradually replaced the old aristocratic mentality. Art, which under the Shang and the early Zhou had been essentially religious, tended to become secular. In each fortified capital the royal court had its artists and artisans, just as it had its strategists, politicians and philosophers. During that period of general upheaval, wars and discoveries led China to become an empire. The process was completed by the outlying state of Qin, which was prepared for its role by a strong political framework consolidated by sensible reforms and the military experience acquired through contact with the barbarian tribes of the north-west.

Qin Shi huang di, who unified the empire in 221 B.C., reigned as an autocrat. He organized the provincial administration and the highway system, standardized script, currency, weights and measures, destroyed the classics that linked China with its past, and built the Great Wall, of which some sections already existed, to protect the country from invasion by northern nomads.

In his capital Xianyang (near Sian, in Shânxi) he erected palaces in the style of each of the subject states, thus bringing in builders from all the regions of the China of his day. This policy had an important bearing on the progress of architecture during the Han period.

The Han Empire

The Qin despotism did not last. The harsh laws and colossal public works exhausted workers and treasury alike. A popular uprising split up the empire. But in 206 B.C. the victorious Liu Bang founded the Han dynasty, which governed China until A.D. 220. The new dynasty is traditionally divided into Early Han and Later Han, whose capitals were respectively Changan (now Sian in Shânxi) and Luoyang (in Henan).

The progress of agriculture, the development of irrigation, and the production of iron benefited a class of landed proprietors which had replaced the old nobility that had been broken up by the Qin. Merchants also were enriched by the expansion of domestic trade and later by the policy of foreign conquest. The Han dynasty set up a class system in which the freedom of research enjoyed during the epoch of the Warring States crystallized into a state philosophy under the aegis of Confucius. The Han annexed Nanyue (today the region of Canton), Tonking and North Annam, penetrated Bactria and Sogdia in the face of strong opposition from the Huns, and finally conquered Korea.

At the very beginning of their reign the Han realized that grand architecture was a prerequisite of stable government and might become an instrument of power. From then on architecture and decoration grew so important that for the first time they became major subjects of literature.

The great advance in building techniques was due to innovations introduced after the epoch of the Warring States, to regional traditions, and to the synthesis of earlier ideas. It was under the Han that the principles of axiality and of timber structures with pillars, beams and brackets were formulated.

The state was everywhere and the system thus created became the ideal that all later dynasties sought to attain. Nonetheless, undermined by court intrigues and peasant revolts, the Han dynasty collapsed in A.D. 220. The country was immediately partitioned and unity was not restored until 589. The north was invaded by nomad tribes that set up new states, while the Chinese sought refuge in the south, establishing kingdoms in the lower Yanzi valley where agriculture, trade and handicrafts thrived amazingly.

During those troublous times, known as the Three Kingdoms and the Six Dynasties, Chinese society was completely transformed. The feudal system was restored and the contrast became more strident between the luxury of the local courts and the misery of a peasantry menaced by invasion, pillage and civil war. But man's need for hope was fed by Taoism and Buddhism. The latter, introduced under the Han, spread throughout the whole empire. It led to the development of buildings in brick and stone and to the erection of innumerable monasteries and temples in towns and countryside after the fifth century. Sanctuaries were cut in the rock in Ganzu, Sichuan, Shânxi, Henan and as far as Shandong in the east and Jiangsu in the south.

The Sui and Tang Dynasties

The empire was reunited by the Sui dynasty (589–618). The brief transition period before consolidation by the Tang was marked by a frenzy of building activity. The Grand Canal between Luoyang and Yangzhou enabled the cereals produced in the regions of the lower Yanzi to reach the old centres of consumption along the middle reaches of the Yellow River. The Emperor Yang di built forty palaces on the banks of the canal and so embellished the city of Yangzhou that it even rivalled the capital. This mania for building, stimulated by Buddhism and the vast programmes due to frequent changes in the site of the capital, reached an unprecedented level under the Tang dynasty.

Lasting as it did from 618 to 907, that period was one of the most glorious in Chinese history and indeed one of the most brilliant civilizations the world has ever seen. During the seventh and eighth centuries of our era China, having recovered her hegemony over Central Asia and Korea, was the most powerful state in the whole continent. Trade prospered and the capital Changan was the most cosmopolitan city in the world. Buddhism was at its apogee, but building activity resulted in excessive deforestation and a shortage of metals, beside placing a heavy burden on the peasantry. Architecture flourished and there was an extraordinary renaissance in every cultural sphere – literature, music and the visual arts.

But symptoms of weakening of the central power appeared in the mid-eighth century and Changan was sacked by Tibetan raiders in 763. The dynasty was un-

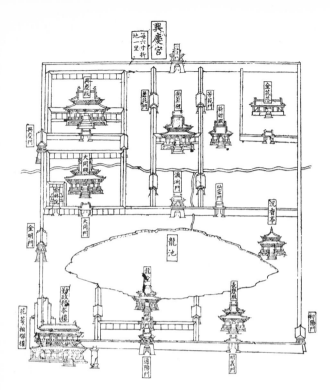

Plan of the Xingqing Palace erected at Changan in 714, from the rubbing of a stele engraved in 1080. In the centre, the oval Dragon's Pool surrounded by pavilions; round about, the halls and gates of the palace

able to check the forces that threatened the unity of the empire, and its dissolution at the beginning of the tenth century left China in a state of military and economic collapse. For half a century the country was a prey to anarchy, split up into several independent kingdoms in both the north and the south.

In the north-east the Khitan Mongols transformed their tribal society into a hereditary monarchy and in 937 set up the Liao kingdom around what is now Peking. Their claim to sovereignty over all China, which was taken up by their successors the Jurchen, who reigned under the dynastic name of Jin after 1124, was a growing threat to the empire from the north.

The Song Dynasty

The dichotomy between the north-east occupied by the barbarians and China proper during the Five Dynasties period (907–960) continued under the Song (960–1279). The situation worsened after 1126, when the Jin captured the capital Kaifeng and the Chinese dynasty was forced to seek refuge first in Nanking and later in Hangzhou, leaving the entire northern portion of the country to the barbarians. China only recovered its unity, though not its independence, in the thirteenth century as a result of the lightning advance of the Mongols under Genghis Khan, who destroyed the Jin kingdom, established their capital at Peking in 1260 and took Hangzhou in 1276.

One of the gates of Kaifeng, capital of the Northern Song (960–1126), from the 'Qing ming shang he tu' scroll in the Imperial Palace Museum, Peking

The Song period was one of consolidation after the great expansion under the Tang. The major features of the Song culture were the growth of cities, the prosperity of the merchant class, the spread of printing, the development of science and technology, the supremacy of the mandarins, the blossoming of literature and landscape painting. In the architectural sphere the Song developed and refined the simpler, homelier style of the Tang. This was characterized by improvement of the timber framework, more use of decoration, curved roofs and increased height.

In North China the Liao evolved a hybrid style based on the Tang tradition. It was marked by an imposing solidity but also by a grandiloquence and complexity that were sometimes oppressive. The Jin discovered Chinese art through the intermediary of the Liao but, since they occupied a far vaster territory in China proper, they found at Kaifeng the finest achievements of the Northern Song (960–1126). Their own architecture followed along the same lines.

China from the Mongols to the Manchus

Genghis Khan's grandson Kublai, who gave his dynasty the name of Yuan (1279–1368), promoted agriculture in North China while leaving the land to its owners in the south. Despite the completion of the great canal that linked the Yanzi to Peking the two regions maintained different social and economic structures. The capital became the centre of all the trade routes of the Mongol empire. Merchants, scholars, officials and monks from the Middle East, Russia and Central Asia obtained posts in the central administration side by side with Chinese collaborators. Even Europeans lived at the Chinese court, the most famous being Marco Polo, who arrived in China in 1275 and did not return home to Venice until twenty years later.

Architecture felt the impact of foreign influences. Kublai commissioned an Arab to build the palaces at Peking with the assistance of a Chinese and a Nepalese for the sculpture. The result was a greater use of stone for terraces, balustrades and gateways, which continued under the Ming and Qing. The arrival of Tibetan lamas in Peking in 1267 influenced religious art by introducing to North China the lamasery style and a new type of pagoda.

At the end of the fourteenth century, taking advantage of the troubles that upset the realm, a peasant founded a new dynasty which took the name of Ming (1368–1644). The Mongols were driven back behind the Great Wall, which was restored, and the capital, first set up in Nanking, was transferred to Peking early in the fifteenth century. The first two Ming emperors displayed great qualities, reorganizing the economy, strengthening the central power and engaging in a policy of expansion. But their successors reigned ingloriously, leaving power in the hands of eunuchs and encouraging a strict Confucianism that ended up by ossifying the mandarin class. On the other hand, the growth of the moneyed middle class thanks to the development of private trade promoted new literary genres, such as the novel and the drama.

Architectural activity under the Ming, though flourishing, brought with it few major innovations. One observes a greater monumentality, stricter symmetry in the ground plan, a larger use of brick and masonry, and a marked taste for horizontality. But architects did little more than copy and embellish traditional forms.

The weakness of the last Ming emperors permitted the leaders of a Tungus tribe that had settled in eastern Manchuria since the beginning of the seventeenth century to invade China. Under the dynastic name of Qing these Manchus held sway for three centuries (1644–1911). They chose Peking as their capital and were well advised in making as few changes as possible in existing institutions.

During the Kang xi (1662–1772), Yong Zheng (1723 to 1735) and Qian long (1735–1772) reigns the empire enjoyed a period of considerable prosperity, though population increased from 140 million at the end of the Ming dynasty to 300 million in 1787. But by the end of the eighteenth century population was increasing faster than production, and by then the Manchu rulers had become steadily weaker. As a result, European designs on the Chinese empire became more and more threatening.

The architectural style developed under the Ming was continued without much imagination under the

A small town in Southern China in the reign of the Emperor Qian long (18th century), from 'Essai sur les mœurs des Chinois, par les Jésuites de Pékin', in Geneva Municipal Library

Qing, who tended towards exaggerated decoration, greater complication, and a taste for the grandiose which, as Jankélévitch said, is 'the sublimity of decadence'. Thus from the sixteenth century to the nineteenth Chinese architecture declined – with a few memorable exceptions – the art and science of building being overshaded by the spurious boldness of corrupt ornamentation.

The Organization of Space

In the ancient Chinese cosmology, which considered Heaven round and Earth square, space is imagined as a series of imbricated squares. The centre of this 'ranked' space is the capital – a square core marked by four gates at the four cardinal points towards which the cosmic influences converge. This leads to a geometrical image of the universe, enlivened by an elementary network of spatial correspondences. The alternations and contrasts of opposites inherent in this notion of the universe are repeated in the human space, where everything is ideally determined by the same total order. Chinese architecture, which was viewed as the crystallization of this harmony, incorporates some essential principles of the ancient theories, such as orientation, pure geometrical forms, and a symmetry that mirrors the alternation of summer and winter, day and night.

Architectural space is like a series of closed worlds, of complete independent, progressively smaller units –from the town to the private house–which repeat on a reduced scale the forms of the larger units. A house may be viewed as a town in miniature; the town as a house on a vast scale. This conception matches on the moral and social plane the supreme importance of balanced overlapping relationships between individual and family, human order and cosmic order. This interplay of relationships strengthens the independent family cells, just as the symbolic organization of space harmonizes the architectural units. In practice, each community–whether town or household–enjoys great autonomy, but this decentralization is never a symptom of anarchy. In China the arrangement of space has always been governed by laws. Architecture has always been an art guided and controlled by the state, aimed not only at organizing the environment but also at providing a frame for the social system. The size of a building, its internal arrangement and its architectural decoration were already determined by the owner's social position as early as the Zhou dynasty (eleventh to third centuries B.C.).

Orientation and Axiality

The concept of order and harmony in the universe is reflected in the many complex rules that governed the siting of an edifice. Geomancers well versed in 'feng-shui' (literally, 'wind and water') were consulted to find out if the lie of the land and the arrangement of trees, rocks and waters were favourable to the good

spirits and capable of keeping away the evil ones.

When the site was decided the architect drew the plan, bearing in mind the main south-north axis. The symbolism of this axiality is obvious. For the Chinese north represented the rigours of winter and the threat of barbarian invasion–namely, evil influences. Hence all important buildings, public or private, opened towards the south. This axiality implied a median avenue and the gradual discovery of the architectural complex as one advanced along it. That complex, whether town or palace, was never designed to be grasped at first glance but only through an approach in space and time, like a piece of music or a scroll painting. The major buildings followed each other along the median axis, preceded by vast courtyards closed on the east and west by buildings of secondary importance.

There was a definite trend towards horizontality, particularly in Northern China, but the status of a monument was not, as in the west, stressed by its commanding position. The Chinese were quite capable of erecting tall buildings. This is proved by the development of multi-storeyed houses towards the beginning of our era and later by the construction of Buddhist pagodas. But preference for a uniform height was linked with the notion of juxtaposed spaces. The main building was distinguished by its site (as a rule, at the far end, facing the entrance), its area, its more costly materials and more refined decoration.

The Plan: the Closed Courtyard

There were three different ways of arranging the architectural ensemble around the south-north axis. The first and perhaps earliest consisted of four buildings surrounding a courtyard, which was often square. This symmetrical arrangement already existed during the Han period (third century B.C. to third century A.D.) and continued virtually unchanged until the nineteenth century. Its application was universal because for large ensembles (palaces, monasteries and the like) it could be multiplied at will.

The second way was symmetrical relative to the south-north axis and entirely enclosed by a wall. This arrangement, which reflected a dualistic conception of the universe, was chosen for the tombs of the Ming emperors and for the Temple of Heaven in Peking.

The third, as exemplified by the Imperial Palace in Peking, was a combination of the other two.

These three options were based on a constant factor probably dating from the feudal society of the first millenary B.C. – in a courtyard closed on all four sides which was the image of a square space, of the complete, independent world I have already mentioned.

Perenniality of Types – Ephemerality of Materials

This repetition on different scales of a single invariable plan resulted in a great stability of structural types. The most frequent unit is a rectangular pavilion (dian), usually divided by cylindrical pillars into three or more transverse naves. Frequently the first of these naves forms a portico, except where a colonnade frames the whole building, which may be square, polygonal or circular. The few variants of this simple plan are obtained by raising the terrace on which the pavilion stands, by multiplying the number of storeys, or by a combination of the two.

As we shall see later, the edifice itself is less important than the terrace that supports it and the roof that covers it. Between these two essential elements – symbols respectively of earth and heaven – the walls do not perform a supporting function. In fact, since the ensemble is always protected by a surrounding wall, those of each building serve only to protect it from the weather. In this respect China was prepared by its architectural tradition to adopt modern materials and techniques.

Structures of this type (pavilions with one or more storeys, towers, kiosks, etc.) were equally well suited for palaces, temples or private dwellings. They were built of timber and destined to be rebuilt by each generation to meet its needs. The preference for timber matched an original conception of architecture; it did not derive from any lack of other materials or of the ability to handle them. In fact, we must not forget that there was also a tradition of building in brick and stone, reserved for bridges, ramparts, terraces, pavements, tombs and certain pagodas.

This preference may have been due partly to the frequent earthquakes, which demanded a flexible structure. But it had its disadvantages. The gradual disappearance of forests and the quantity of highly skilled labour it involved made timber construction so costly that after the twelfth or thirteenth century steps had to be taken to economize materials. Another serious drawback was the risk of fire. The Japanese monk Ennin relates in his travelogue that 4,000 houses were destroyed by a fire which broke out in the eastern market of Changan in 843. There are many other reports of the same kind. But reconstruction was no less rapid than the cataclysms were violent, and the authorities did not expect buildings to last much more than a generation.

This deliberately ephemeral architecture, whose products were not destined to defy time, is explained by the fact that China has never linked its destiny with the transient fate of its material realizations. It views history as a predestined, inevitable sequence of events, in which the various moments count less than a certain coherent continuity. Each great dynasty started out with the idea of restoring the situation that had existed under its predecessor. Its first steps were conservative and several generations passed before original achievements appeared. The same principle applied to architecture. It was not in their monuments that the Chinese expressed their passion for eternity but in the ideas that presided over their design and the spiritual tradition they exemplified.

Chinese architecture reflects a certain conception of man's relationship to the universe. It draws no fundamental difference in respect of materials and methods, shapes and styles, between public and private or between secular and religious edifices. I shall attempt to trace, proceeding from the town to the dwelling, from the macrocosm to the microcosm, some of the major achievements of that art, ending up with its antidote to order and symmetry – the art of gardening, which aims at integrating man in nature.

Plates

Chinese Landscapes

17 Curiously shaped peaks rise on both banks of the River Li in the Guilin region of Guangxi.

18 Terraced tillage in the Yan an region, Shânxi. The layout of the fields on the sides of the loess hills shows how cleverly the Chinese adapted to the natural lines of the country.

19 Flooded paddy-fields in the south of Henan province.

20 Fish-ponds on Lake Taihu near Wuxi, Jiangsu. The regular layout recalls the division of a city into blocks.

The Great Wall

21 Today the Great Wall stretches from the River Yalu in the east to the Jiayu Pass in Gansu. This work, which served both for defence and communication, dates from the Ming period (1368–1644).

22– The ramparts that developed into the Great Wall
23 were built during the Warring States epoch (fifth to third centuries B.C.) by the states of Northern China. They were prolonged by the Qin (221–06 B.C.) for defence against the increasingly dangerous Xiongnu horsemen.

24 Guard-house on the Great Wall.

25 The Great Wall played more than a merely military role. It was a means of communication through inhospitable mountainous regions; it also served to settle soldier-colonists in the bordering non-Han regions and helped to control the movements of the nomad tribes.

26 The Great Wall, which follows the lines of the ridges, seems to complete the massive landscape of China's northern frontier.

27 Here the building procedure is clear to see: rubble walls faced with stone topped by a brick-paved roadway edged with parapet and battlements.

28 The Juyong Passage, entrance to the Great Wall northeast of Peking. The magnificent stone gatehouse dates from the Yuan period (1342–45). It is built to a square plan. The canted arch is embellished with marble bas-reliefs representing the Buddha and his four heavenly guardians.

Peking: The Imperial City: the Walls

29 The Qian men as it is today. The outer tower is the only one still standing. Located on the great south-north axis, it used to link the Imperial City to the north and the Outer City to the south.

30 The walls of Peking, like a frame, enclose and limit the Chinese city. They are its most essential and permanent feature.

31 The north wall of Peking. Its ponderous rhythm is stressed by the mighty bastions that rise along it at regular intervals.

Bridges

32 A stone bridge over a small canal at Suzhou, Jiangsu province. The city lies east of Lake Taihu on the banks of the former Grand Canal.

33 The Luguo qiao, south-west of Peking, which Europeans call the Marco Polo Bridge, was built between 1189 and 1192. Its eleven arches have voussoirs about 3 feet thick.

34 The Baodai qiao (Bridge of the Precious Girdle) in the southern suburb of Suzhou is over 100 yards long. Its three central arches are higher in order to let boats pass through.

35 a) The Pavilion Bridge on a branch of the Grand Canal in the south-west quarter of Suzhou (Jiangsu). It has three stone arches, of which the middle one is topped by a pavilion.
b) Bridge on Tortoise-head Peninsula on Lake Taihu at Wuxi (Jiangsu)

36 The splendid seventeen-arch bridge of the Summer Palace north-west of Peking. It connects Langwang miao Island in Lake Kunming to the mainland.

◀ Plans

Notes

Some Problems of Urban Population Distribution from the Han to the Ming

The cities of the Former Han were divided into quarters (li) and seem to have been market towns formed by a number of adjacent villages. At that time, in fact, the character 'li' designated a village, a city quarter and a measure of length and area. This last meaning proves that in the cities the 'li' were originally plots allotted by the state. The Han must have used the division into 'li' to maintain the village organization that enabled them to keep a check on the mainly agricultural population. Actually there does not seem to have been either opposition or precise demarcation between town and country at that time.

This Former Han city, from being populated chiefly by agricultural workers, developed gradually into the agglomerate of urban population of the Tang period. This evolution had already started under the Later Han, but social upheavals, migrations and agrarian reforms during the troublous times of the Six Dynasties probably went far towards destroying the 'li' system.

Under the Tang the division into blocks (fang) was already less strict. Mutual supervision – and mutual solidarity too, for that matter – was organized in a town or village by distributing the population in groups of five households (bao). Each household of a 'bao' was co-responsible for the behaviour of the four others and for that of the neighbouring households. What is more, each block – like each village – was ruled by a headman authorized to represent it in dealings with the administration. These units enjoyed a certain autonomy and community life was centred in the blocks, whose inhabitants were linked by bonds of family, religion or calling. Thus the city area was made up of a quantity of small self-contained social cells that were independent to some extent of the hierarchized network of the government agencies.

The growth of the cities under the Tang and the extraordinary economic expansion under the Song disrupted the urban system and did away with walled blocks and with fixed, closed markets. But the trading cities of the twelfth and thirteenth centuries did not make any visible change in the political system or achieve true urban autonomy. Under the Ming the blocks were restored and there was a pause in urban growth. This was due to the small size of the only coherent human units (the inhabitants of the same block, the members of the same corporation). It was also due to 'the administrative hierarchy that embraced it.' (J. Gernet, 'La ville chinoise au moment de l'apogée islamique', in L'Année sociologique, Vol. 17/1966.) Local society, with its limited range of relationships, was ruled from above by a government machine whose complexity increased with the growth of the economy and which failed to create the charters, the legal guarantees, the franchises and the privileges indispensable for the free development of urban activities.

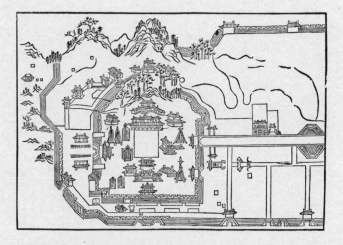

Plan of the imperial city of Hangzhou in the thirteenth century, with its wall pierced by gates and its palace quarter in the middle, from an ancient Chinese document.

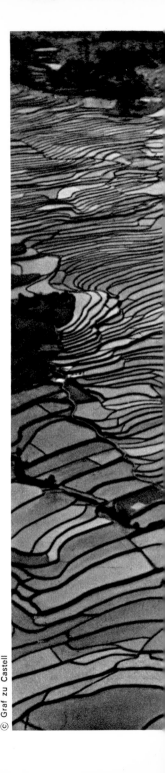

18

30

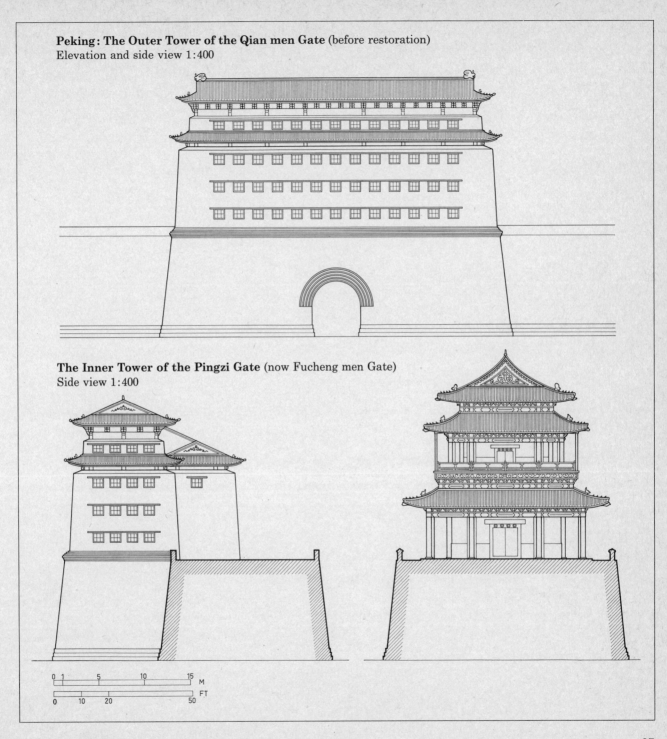

Peking: The Outer Tower of the Qian men Gate (before restoration)
Elevation and side view 1:400

The Inner Tower of the Pingzi Gate (now Fucheng men Gate)
Side view 1:400

0 1 5 10 15 M
0 10 20 50 FT

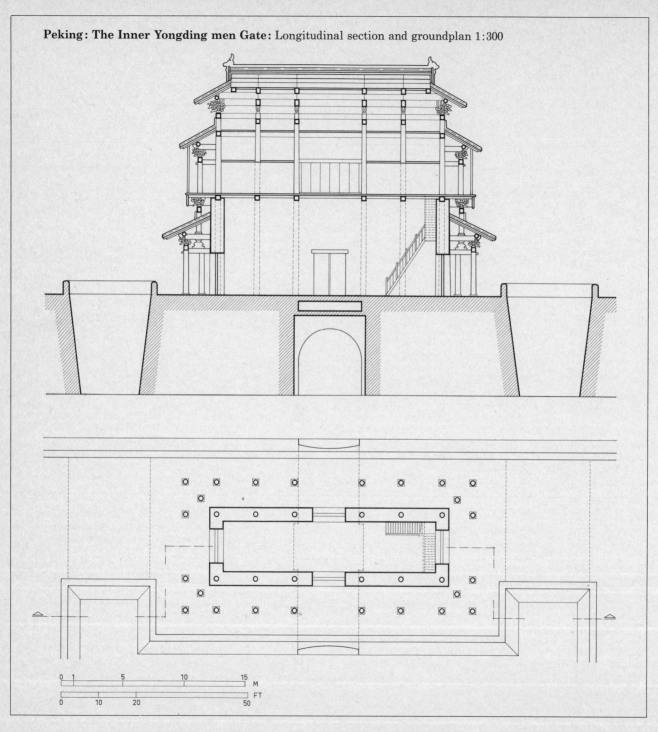

Peking: The Inner Yongding men Gate: Longitudinal section and groundplan 1:300

2. Town Planning

Chinese architectural concepts are indissolubly linked with a social order at once real and ideal, with a structured vision of the universe and with a certain scale of values. They are best crystallized in town planning.

Ancient texts give us an idea of how a city was established. The founder began by inspecting the region. To determine its orientation 'he observes the shadows, examines the sunny and dark sides, the "yang" and "yin" of the country to see how the constituent principles of the world are distributed. Lastly, he finds out the direction in which the waters flow. It is he who must realize the religious value of the site (what was later called "feng sui")', says Marcel Granet in 'La Civilisation Chinoise' (Paris 1948).

In addition to these geomantic preoccupations, which played a decisive role all through Chinese history, the founder's choice was also governed by practical considerations (supplies of food and water, facilities for defence, means of communication, the availability of skilled labour) and cultural factors, first among them the mythical and historical value of the site.

Once the site was chosen and the propitious moment for starting work was fixed, first the ramparts – the most sacred part of a city – were erected, then the temple of the ancestors, and finally the palaces and dwelling houses.

The most ancient rules of Chinese town planning (those of the Zhou li or 'Zhou Rituals') aimed at making the city a cosmos – a true image of the universe as an ordered whole. This pursuit of harmony explains the great importance of orientation. The ideal capital was a quadrilateral girt round with walls pierced by twelve gates corresponding to the twelve months of the year. The royal residence, also square and walled, lay in the centre like a city within the city. Each edifice had its proper place. In the middle, the audience hall opened on a road that passed between the Altar of the Sun and the Temple of the Ancestors and ended at the South Gate. This avenue was used by the processions of vassals on their way to pay homage to the prince, who sat facing south. Situated at the very heart of the city and, symbolically, at the heart of the universe, the palace faced south and turned its back on the market, which was located at the northernmost edge of the enclosure, an inferior position reflecting the status of trade and commerce (except in Changan of the Tang).

The orientation of the Chinese city, with its geometrical plan, its chief axes from south to north and from east to west, recalls that of the Roman civitas. But the Chinese plan was centred round the prince, ruler of the world and pivot of the universe, or his provincial representative. Instead, the centre of the Roman city was the forum, symbol of the interests of the citizens, their rights and the part they played in civil and religious affairs. On the sociological plane this contrast may be explained by the fact that in China a townsman was not considered a citizen but a subject. The capital was not his home but a temporary residence, a centre of business and government, where he stayed only as long as good fortune permitted.

The south-north and east-west avenues that divided the city into blocks performed a function of social control. Each block was surrounded by walls and formed a self-contained little city, the unit for census and recruitment for forced labour and military service. As it consisted of a quantity of closed cells, the city had no open centre for civic activity like the agora, the forum or the crossroads. Rather were its architectural features strung out along an axis in a given direction. This principal avenue, which did duty as a triumphal way, was far from being a continuous succession of buildings. The administrative enclosure containing the royal residences and the government offices always formed a hiatus. The officials who had an entry to the Imperial Palace were not free to come and go as they pleased. Some could go only to certain offices, others only to the servants' quarters; and their points of entry were rigidly prescribed. In Peking the Triumphal Way was not thrown open to the public until the fall of the empire in 1912.

The Chinese city was designed by administrators for administrators and built as a rule by conscripted labour. It was planned on a grander scale than any western state could undertake from the decline of Rome to the industrial revolution of the nineteenth century. And the area and population of Chinese cities were far greater than those of European towns of the same period.

- Luoyang (6th century): 500,000 inhabitants,
- Nanking (6th century): 1 million inhabitants,
- Changan (7th–10th centuries): over 1 million inhabitants,
- Hangzhou (1275): 1 million inhabitants,
- Peking (late 18th century): 2 or 3 million inhabitants,

compared with
- Paris (12th century): 100,000 inhabitants,
- Constantinople (1453): 180,000 inhabitants,
- Paris (15th century): 200,000 inhabitants,
- Venice (early 15th century): about 200,000 inhabitants,
- Paris (1784): 620,000 inhabitants.

The importance of urban agglomerations in a pre-industrial economy may have been due to the bureaucratic organization of Chinese society. But also to the fact that in China a balance was achieved at a very early date between town and country, the former often acting as granary and storehouse for the latter. Most of the traditional centres were either market towns that supplied the needs of the surrounding rural communities or administrative cities conditioned by political or military considerations that were subject to change. This explains why the capital was shifted relatively often. It was easy to rebuild a city, copying what was already there, either on the accession of a new dynasty or for demographic reasons. Both Peking and Changan are classic examples of the re-utilization of a site and its remodelling on the scale of an administrative city in the course of centuries. Hence the city was a collective achievement, whose unity was due to the tradition on which its plan was based and to a monumental view of the whole rather than of a few major edifices. As we have already seen, no edifice dominated the others, and the ramparts, gates and corner towers were the tallest, most massive features. This stresses that defence was the essential function of the Chinese city, which was first and foremost a bastion against barbarian attacks and any other disorders that might threaten the harmonious organization of the world.

The Origin of the Cities

The need to defend and fortify the villages by surrounding them with a rampart of rammed earth was first felt in China at the end of the Neolithic Period.

The earliest Shang city we know of is Zhengzhou (Henan), which might be the Shang capital Ao (c. sixteenth to fourteenth centuries B.C.). It occupied a rectangular area of about 7,500 acres and was surrounded by a wall in layers of rammed earth each 3–4 inches thick. The city seems to have been chiefly an administrative and religious centre. The ruling aristocracy lived inside the walls, the craftsmen (iron workers, potters, sculptors) and peasants in the suburbs. The second capital so far excavated is Anyang (also in Henan), which was inhabited from the fourteenth to the eleventh centuries B.C. It is a very homogeneous complex with the same features as Zhengzhou. The site lies on the banks of the Huan River. The city stood on the south bank, leaving the north bank for burials. The Shang capital, the nerve centre of the kingdom over which it held political and economic sway, was protected by its ramparts and contained the granaries and the royal treasury. It was the residence of the king, the priests and the court dignitaries, who were ministered to by a host of servants, artisans and farmers.

The Shang traditions were apparently maintained by the Western Zhou at the beginning of the first millenium B.C. but traces of a city dating from that period have not yet been discovered. There seems to have been a change at the beginning of the Eastern Zhou dynasty (seventh–sixth centuries B.C.). The number of cities increased with the rise of provincial states. Many of these feudal cities have been excavated. In 1957–8 an ancient walled city was discovered at Houma, in southern Shânxi, which may have been Xintian capital of Jin state (sixth–fifth centuries B.C.). The city was rather small and boasted few palaces; the craftsmen's quarters lay outside the walls. During the same period Linzi (Qi state) in Shandong, a very large city with 70,000 families, had its craftsmen's quarters inside the walls.

Handan (Zhao state) in Hebei brings us to the fourth century. The site, unfortunately incomplete, is square and has sixteen rammed-earth platforms, the most important of which is over 44 feet high.

Xiadu (Yan state) in Hebei, one of the most famous cities of the Warring States, is slightly later. It was excavated in 1961–2. The walls measure about 12 miles in perimeter. The rectangular city is divided into two square parts to the west and east of a canal that served to transport grain. Traces of four gates, of roads and of canals have been discovered. The eastern city, where most of the cultural relics were found, has terraces – the palace stood on one –, traces of workshops (potters, armourers, toolmakers, coiners and bone-carvers) and housing quarters (to the south-west). The north-east section of eastern Xiadu was occupied by the royal tombs.

Diggings on these sites have revealed that both cities and palaces grew larger from the sixth to the second century. One is led to draw the following conclusions.

1. All cities were enclosed by walls of rammed earth. After digging a shallow foundation trench, the labourers heaped up the earth between planks placed on edge to form a long casing supported by stakes. They packed the earth very tight before starting on the next course. Each course was 2–3 inches thick and the whole wall varied in width from 15 to 50 feet. Gateways were strengthened with towers, enclosing a parade ground and forming a redan.
2. Most cities were square or rectangular. The city and the official buildings were oriented towards the cardinal points, with special emphasis on the north-south axis.
3. All buildings used for political or religious purposes stood on platforms of rammed earth.
4. A constant feature was the existence of specialized districts, in accordance with the Chinese principle of social segregation.

The Shang city was a religious and administrative enclosure reserved for the aristocracy, which was thus distinguished from the rest of the community. A change occurred towards the sixth century. Alongside the walled enclosure reserved for the aristocracy, a larger area comprising artisan districts, resi-

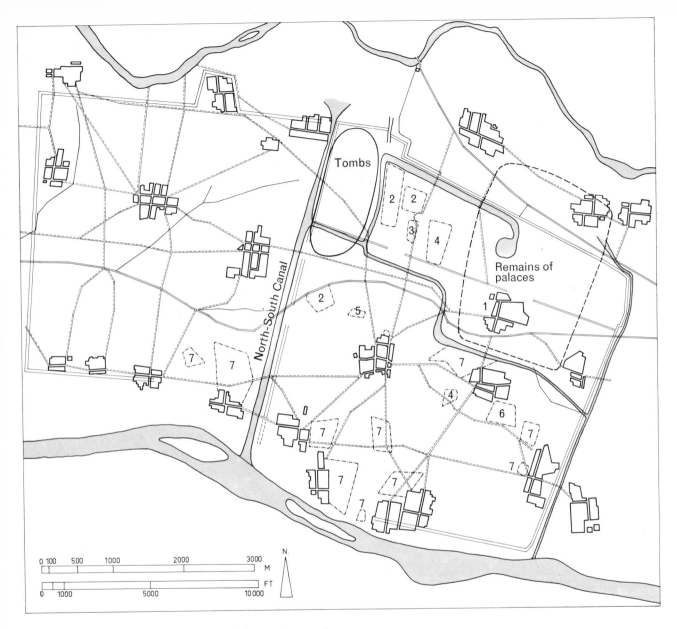

Plan of the remains of the ancient city of Xiadu (Yan State)
at Jixian, Hebei

1 Wuyang terrace, centre of the palace zone
2 Iron-smelters' workshops
3 Bone-carvers' workshops

4 Armourers' workshops
5 Coin-casters' shops
6 Potters' kilns
7 Major remains of urban dwellings

dential districts and shopping streets was also surrounded by a rampart. From then on the city was made up of three distinct spatial units:

1. an enclosure reserved for the aristocracy;
2. the artisan and merchant districts in a larger enclosure;
3. tilled fields outside the ramparts.

This new formula symbolized the growing importance and specialization of the artisan class, whose quarters were under the protection and control of the fortified city. On this point historical texts confirm the results of diggings and tell us that one could purchase jewelry, leather goods, textiles, salt, medicines and art objects in the shops of the cities, which also contained inns, taverns, brothels and gambling dens. The increasing thickness of the walls, which were often reinforced by moats, proves that the need for defence was also on the increase.

The Qin and the Han
(third century B.C. to third century A.D.)

The empire unified under Qin Shih huang di and later under the Han dynasty profited by the innovations introduced during the feudal period. After his definitive victory in 221 B.C. Qin Shih huang di transferred 120,000 of the wealthiest and most powerful families in the empire to his capital Xianyang in Shânxi. Whenever he conquered a territory he built at Xianyang a replica of the palace he had demolished, adorned it with the treasures he had seized, and lodged there the women taken from the vanquished foe. The number of palaces and pavilions of this type reproduced in his capital totalled 145.

On seizing power in 206 B.C. the Han re-utilized many of the cities of the Warring States and founded new ones to suit the recent administrative division of the empire.

The typical agglomeration of the period was encircled by walls pierced by gates on the four sides. The city inside the walls was divided into several districts separated by streets or avenues. Each district was surrounded by its own wall, which had a single gateway and comprised some hundred houses, each in its own enclosure. These houses were reached by narrow streets leading from the one gate of the district. To leave the city, the inhabitants had to pass through at least three gates: the gate of their own house, the gate of the district and the gate of the city. All these gates were guarded by day and closed at night. The system of locking up the population inside walled enclosures facilitated supervision and recruitment.

Every large city had a special district reserved for the market and containing shops. Merchants and craftsmen lived close to this market, whereas agricultural workers lived near the city gates so that they could go out easily to till the land. The administrative buildings were located in the centre of the city.

Plan of the cities that occupied the present Sian (Shânxi) in historical times
1 Feng jing (1122 B.C.)
2 Hao jing
3 Xianyang of the Qin (246 B.C.)
4 Changan of the Han (c. 200 B.C.)
5 Changan of the Sui and Tang (A.D. 581)
6 The Ming city (1390)
7 Sian in 1958

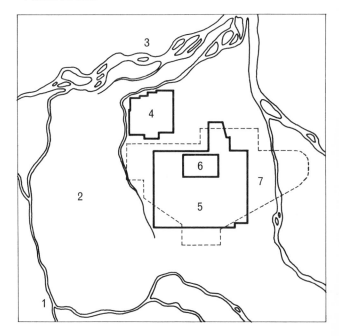

During the Former Han period (206 B.C.–A.D. 9) there seem to have been over 37,000 cities. Their number gradually fell to 17,000 under the Latter Han (A.D. 25–220). This is explained by the increasing importance of the suburbs due to the growth of the population. The cities grew larger and the official policy of centralization led to a concentration of the inhabitants. On the other hand, colonization and clearance of new lands led to the formation of vast estates that took the shape of villages.

Prospecting and excavation on the site of Changan, capital of the Former Han, started in 1956. The city, which occupied a rough square on the south bank of the River Wei, lay to the north-west of the present-day Sian (Shânxi). The ramparts were 15½ miles long, 60 feet high and some 50 feet thick. They were commenced in 192 B.C. and finished three years later. On each side were three gates, each with three openings. The emperor's palace and the homes of the aristocracy seem to have occupied the centre and south of the city – two-thirds of the total area. The north-west section comprised the administrative services and the craftsmen's quarters. The rest of the population lived in the north-east section. There were nine major markets located to the east and west of the city's chief south-north thoroughfare. Changan had 160 enclosed districts, separated by streets that criss-crossed at right angles. This chessboard layout became generalized thenceforth.

The Period of the Great Projects: The Sui and the Tang (589–907)

Luoyang, capital of the Eastern Han, was still a very active centre during the Three Kingdoms and Six Dynasties period. In the sixth century it had 500,000 inhabitants inside a wall that measured 2½ miles from north to south and 1½ from east to west. But the long period of troubles (221–589) following the fall of the Han dynasty did not favour large-scale public works. It was only after the Sui had reunited the empire at the end of the sixth century that grand projects were undertaken. They were completed by the Tang (618–907).

Changan (City of the Long Peace)

When the Sui reunited the empire they decided to build a capital on a scale never seen before. They chose the site of Changan and fixed the plan of the city, which was completed and embellished by the Tang during the first two centuries of their reign.

Changan, which was chosen by the Zhou, Qin and Han as their capital, had many advantages. Not least was the fertile, populous region that encircled it, linked by road with Central Asia, by water with Sichuan to the south and Shandong to the east. Historical precedents counted, too, for the great Chinese dynasties had achieved success when they had been centred on this plain, whose innumerable ancient tombs were so many links with a glorious past. But the Sui wanted to build an entirely new city, so they did not utilize the ruins of the Han city. A new site, to the south-east of the old one, was considered auspicious. On the north and east it was bounded by two rivers, which solved the problem of the water supply.

Though it retained a great many features of the ideal city of the Zhou li, the Changan of the Sui and Tang displayed some novel aspects that were due to two causes.

1. Yu Wenkai (555–612), the most famous architect, engineer and town-planner of the Sui dynasty, was not of 'Han' origin. He found his inspiration in the barbarian capitals erected in Northern China between the third and sixth centuries.
2. In the conception of the city a pragmatic spirit prevailed. The major innovations consisted in locating the palace against the north wall, concentrating the government offices in a walled precinct directly south of the palace, distributing the residential districts to the south, east and west of the palace-government complex, and setting up the two markets where they could best serve as depots for the commodities that reached the city from east and west.

The Plan

The city was built to a basically symmetrical plan, covering an area measuring 6 miles from east to west

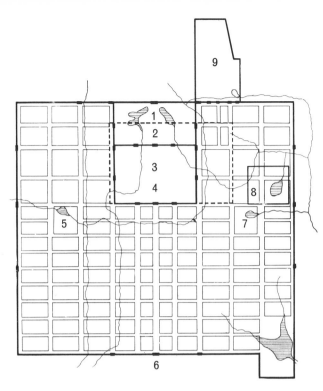

Plan of Changan of the Tang (618–907)

1 Taiji Palace
2 Chengdian Gate
3 Imperial City
4 Zhujue Gate
5 West Market
6 Mingde Gate
7 East Market
8 Xingqing Palace
9 Daming Palace

and 5 miles 3 furlongs from north to south. The walls were 16 feet thick and 22 miles 5 furlongs long. They were pierced by three gates on the south, east and west and eight on the north.

The city was divided into three parts:
– to the extreme north, the imperial palace (3083 yards by 1630 yards) surrounded by a wall of rammed earth 20 yards thick at the base in some places;
– to the south of the palace, the imperial city (3083 yards by 2015 yards) containing the government buildings and their appendages;
– the outer city, which surrounded the other two on the south, east and west.

Thus the imperial palace and the government buildings were entirely separate from the markets and the districts where the common people lived. In addition, the imperial city, besides being enclosed by a wall on the east, west and south, was separated from the palace by an avenue 253 yards wide.

The south-north axis led from the Mingde Gate (with five openings) in the centre of the south wall, through the Zhujue Gate of the imperial city, to the Chengdian Gate of the palace. This avenue was 165–70 yards wide and edged at each side by a canal 10 feet wide. Brick-paved streets over 110 yards wide parallel to the main axis led to the other gates of the imperial city.

The Block System

The block system is one of the characteristic features of the Tang city. The south-north axis cut the outer city into two sections – east and west – each of which had its own administration and police. The whole area was divided into 108 square or rectangular blocks by eleven south-north and fourteen east-west avenues. The great poet Bai Juyi (776–846) speaks of this chessboard arrangement:

'Ten thousand houses are like a game of chess,
The Streets are like market garden lots.'

Each block (fang) was enclosed by its own wall. The smallest measured about 6 acres and had two gates, one to the east and one to the west, linked by a wide street. The largest covered twice or even four times that area and had four gates linked by two avenues at right angles. The gates of the blocks were closed at nightfall and the unlighted streets were deserted.

Each of these fang comprised dwelling houses and temples. They accommodated officials, landed proprietors, monks, merchants, artisans and a host of foreigners. Half a block, or even a whole block, was often occupied by a monastery. The streets and avenues, which ranged from 22 to 44 yards wide, were planted with trees. In the south-east corner of the city a park laid out round a lake offered the townspeople kiosks, pavilions and walks. But it was only open to the public on feast days: the rest of the year it was reserved for the imperial family and the aristocracy.

The Markets

The east and west markets, which were the centres of crafts and trade, occupied two blocks each along a line parallel to the imperial city. Four roads at right angles divided each market into nine squares. The administrative offices that checked units of measurement, fixed prices and levied taxes occupied the central square.

The two markets comprised 220 trading units. Trading was opened at noon by 300 drum-beats and closed by 300 strokes of the bell 1¾ hours before sunset. Special locations were reserved for the booths of merchants in the same line of business and the workshops of craftsmen of the same trade. Each corporation had its own street (hang, which in the eighth century began to denote guild or corporation). Excavations on the site of the south street of the west market have yielded a quantity of Tang coins, toilet articles, beads and ornaments in agate and crystal. This west market (1,013 × 1,127 yards) had streets bordered by open drains. The jewelry and wine shops that lined it were kept by merchants from Central and Western Asia. Sassanid coins and gold coins of the Eastern Roman Empire found in the tombs of the period prove that Changan was a centre of foreign trade.

The plan of the vast capital served as a model for many other cities both Chinese, like Luoyang (Henan), and foreign, like Nara, the Japanese capital founded in 710. Changan was conceived on the scale of the continent it governed. At the end of the sixth century a million people lived within its walls. They were distributed very irregularly since some blocks were occupied by fields, drill squares, polo grounds and the ornamental parks that surrounded the houses of the aristocracy. The liveliest quarters were those close to the two markets. It was there that the few multi-storeyed buildings stood: mostly tea-houses and eating places.

Changan and Luoyang, which was rebuilt under the Sui and the Tang to the west of the site occupied during the sixth century, were not the only great Tang cities that have been traced. There are also the trading centres of the Yanzi basin, such as Yangzhou (Jiangsu) to the east and Chengdu (Sichuan) to the west. Temporary markets formed by open-air displays at the crossroads of important trade routes developed into permanent settlements. This is the origin of the trade centres of the Song dynasty.

The Song Dynasty (960–1279)

In the tenth century a series of new developments changed the face of the Chinese city.
– Barbarian pressure led to the closing of the Central Asian trade routes, the rise of the great states of Xixia, Liao and Jin, and the removal of the routes and capitals to the east. The Song emperors took up their residence at Kaifeng, supplied by water from the south-east, whereas Changan turned towards Central Asia and was supplied chiefly by road. This phenomenon was still more in evidence after the capital was transferred to Hangzhou, half-way between the great seaports and the Yanzi valley.
– Advances in agricultural techniques led to an increase in population, which grew from 60 million in 1060 to 100 million in 1170.
– The new fiscal system, based on trade taxes (on salt, tea, etc.), encouraged trade in cereals, while the development of a monetary economy promoted the formation of corporations and of great markets outside the walls.

In the cities this involved the breaking-up of the blocks and markets, the development of an urban lower class and of the tertiary sector (distributive activities).

At that time the urban population was concentrated in three major regions – in the north round the capital Kaifeng, in the south-east (Zhejiang and Jiangxi), and in the west (Sichuan). These three regions coincided with the three major economic zones. The two first also comprised the political centres Kaifeng and Hangzhou.

Kaifeng (Henan),
Capital of the Northern Song (960–1126)

Built in 955, Kaifeng covered an area of 8 square miles and was traversed by several waterways. One of these, the River Bian, which was spanned by thirteen bridges, was the chief means of communication by water. Three walled enclosures contained the palace in the centre, the imperial city and the outer city, in that order. Houses of two or three storeys were common sights owing to the demographic explosion. For that reason Song authors called Kaifeng a city of towers. The imperial way, 330 yards wide, was lined by porticoes where merchants were allowed to trade. The Emperor Hui Zong (1101–26) had barriers placed along the avenue in order to reserve the central lane for his own exclusive use. But in 1126 the city was taken by the Jin, who carried off the emperor and 3,000 members of his court as captives. They pillaged the palaces, stripped them of all the precious objects they contained and took with them the artists and craftsmen who worked for the court.

Hangzhou (Zhejiang),
Capital of the Southern Song (1127–1279)

Beautifully located at the southern end of the Grand Canal, between the River Qiantang and the West Lake, Hangzhou was out of range of the barbarian invasions and had the immense economic advantage of lying half-way between the Yanzi valley and the great ports of Fuzhou and Quanzhou on the southeast coast. Yet, despite the charming landscape, this site was not enthusiastically welcomed as the seat of the central government. The Song emperors always hoped to reconquer the north and considered Hangzhou merely as a temporary residence (Xingzai, the name still employed when the city was occupied by the Mongols, which Marco Polo transcribed 'Quinsay'). But, however temporary it was meant to be, the choice of Hangzhou had enormous consequences. Before the arrival of the court, the city was merely the seat of a provincial governor with probably fewer than 200,000 inhabitants. In less than two centuries it became the great economic centre of Southern

China, the richest and largest city in the world. The population grew steadily during that period, from 468,000 inhabitants in 1170 to 1 million in 1275.

In the thirteenth century the whole area within the walls was built up and the population overflowed into the suburbs. Shortage of space and the demographic explosion resulted in the necessity of building houses with up to five storeys. While the southern section of the city, where the nobles, officials and rich mer-

Plan of Hangzhou, Zhejiang, capital of the Southern Song (1127–1279)

1 Imperial Palace 4 Seventh-century wall
2 Imperial Way   5 Outer wall of 893
3 Principal canal

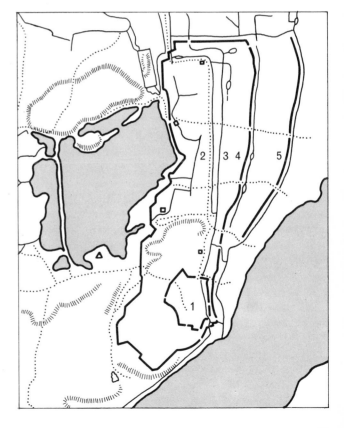

chants lived, was sparsely populated, the people's quarters were so overcrowded that fires frequently broke out, causing great havoc because most of the houses were built of timber: 13,000 houses were destroyed in 1132 and 10,000 in 1137. The city was divided into sectors for fire fighting, with observation towers and military patrols.

Not all the canals that traversed the city and, after passing the walls through five watergates, linked Hangzhou with the nearby prefectures were equally important. Some must have been between 20 and 35 feet wide. In 1271 there were 117 bridges inside the walls and 230 outside. The main avenue, the Imperial Way, was 65 yards wide and over 3 miles long. It was lined with tea-houses, where members of high society learnt to play musical instruments, and luxury shops where foreign commodities and regional products (e.g. silk and flowers from Suzhou) were sold. Nearly all the streets seem to have been paved with large stone slabs. In many of them small shops sold goods of every sort and kind. There were also ten big markets, testifying to the city's intense trading activity. Rice, pork and salt fish, bamboo canes, firewood and timber were imported. The flourishing local craftsmen produced jewelry, artificial flowers, toys, books and porcelain ware. Big merchants who worked for the state made huge fortunes out of salt, spirits and tea, which were government monopolies. This prosperity forced the peasantry to develop market farming and animal husbandry. It also encouraged the development of the entertainment industries – taverns, theatres, restaurants, hotels, caterers, tea-houses and music-halls. The number of public entertainers – jugglers, wrestlers, rope-walkers, conjurers and pedlars – was immense. There were many more prostitutes in the tea-houses and taverns than at Kaifeng. They lived in luxurious houses and kept servants. Parks and gardens skirting the lake and in the southern suburb provided facilities for social gatherings and amusements of all sorts. Hangzhou under the Song was very different from Changan under the Tang. Trade and pleasure-seeking burst the bonds of the traditional system of closed blocks. Night life, of which there had been hardly a trace in the Tang capital, was extremely gay in Hangzhou.

Today, in addition to the magnificent site, the only relics of the thirteenth-century city are the Pagoda of the Six Harmonies (Liuhe ta) and a few vestiges scattered in the hills. But there is no lack of ancient descriptions by Chinese men of letters and Japanese travellers. The most enthusiastic is that of Marco Polo, who visited Hangzhou towards the end of the century. 'There is no other city like it in the world', he wrote, 'nor any that offers such delights that you would think you were in paradise.' I have borrowed the gist of this paragraph from J. Genet's masterly study of life in those times ('La Vie quotidienne en Chine à la veille de l'Invasion mongole, 1250–1276', Paris 1959).

Town Planning under the Yuan, Ming and Qing (1280–1911)

It was under the Yuan dynasty (1280–1368) that the first Drum, Bell and market towers were erected in Chinese cities. Most of those buildings, from which the curfew and night watches were sounded, stood on raised terraces and had two or three storeys with a projecting verandah round the main storey. One of the handsomest is that of Sian (formerly Changan), which dates from the Ming period.

The Yuan, and after them the Ming, reverted to the closed block system that had existed before the Song. They fortified a great many towns and villages for fear of invasion from the north and still more of local peasant uprisings. Within their well protected limits residential quarters developed where the rich merchants built themselves splendid homes. Thus the Chinese cities grew to look as they do today. Those in the north were square or rectangular, with streets intersecting at right angles and in the centre the Drum or Bell Tower. The villages of the plains were surrounded by walls of rammed earth. In the southern agglomerations, on the bank of a river or the flank of a mountain, the plan was less regular and was traversed by canals and streams. In the north, as Prof. O. Sirén has said, the fortifications were the major features of a townscape, and the Chinese could sooner imagine a house without a roof than a town without walls. If this was true of the Tang cities, it was truer

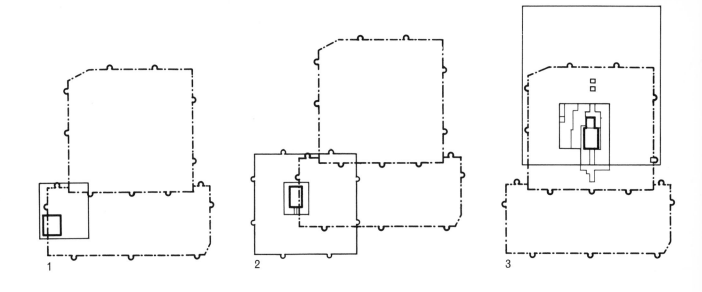

Successive locations of the Liao, Jin and Yuan capitals at Peking. Dotted lines: Peking of the Ming and Qing. Heavy lines: palace sites
1 The Liao capital Yan jing
2 The Jin capital Zhong
3 The Yuan capital Dadu (Khanbalic)

still of those built in the fifteenth century or later, and particularly of Peking, whose layout is a compendium of Chinese town planning.

Peking before the Mongols

Peking is situated at the apex of the great plain dominated by a grandiose arc of mountains (the Yan shan to the north and hills to the west). It was known by the name of Ji during the epoch of the Warring States and became the capital of Yan. At that time it occupied the north-west corner of the present-day Outer City. In the third century B.C. it was destroyed by Qin Shi huang di. After being rebuilt in the first century of our era it was held alternately by Chinese and barbarians as possession of the empire passed from one to the other in the regions close to the Great Wall. In 936 it was captured by the Liao, who made it their southern capital. The Liao city occupied the ancient site and spread towards the west and south. The plan was quadrangular and the palace, surrounded by a double wall, stood in the south-west section. After 1125 the Jin emperors made it their residence and enlarged the city, which they called Zhongdu or Daxingfu, towards the east.

Peking under the Yuan Dynasty

The Mongols conquered the city in 1215 and set fire to the palace, which burnt for thirty days. In 1264 the site became the capital of Mongol China and Kublai took up residence there. A new city founded to the north of the old one was called Dadu (The Great Capital) or Khanbalic (The City of the Khan).

This new city was designed in accordance with the old Chinese principle of 'the imperial court in front, the market at the back' and covered an approximately rectangular area with a perimeter of 16 miles that coincided with the inner city of the Ming dynasty but extended slightly farther towards the north. It was divided into the Palace, the Imperial City and the Outer City. This latter comprised fifty large blocks occupied mostly by the homes of the aristocracy. The shopping district was located to the north-west. The walls were still of rammed earth and in 1359 wooden bridges were thrown over the moat at the eleven city gates. At that same period U-shaped walls were built outside these gates, and towers – probably of brick – were erected over them and at the corners of the wall. Marco Polo wrote that the streets were very broad and straight; 'all the plots on which the houses stand are square and exactly in line with each other. . . . Each square plot is limited by fine, busy streets, so the whole city is laid out in squares like a chessboard and arranged in so perfect and masterly a fashion that no description can possibly do justice to its beauty'. The Drum and Bell Towers (built in 1272) rose in the centre of the city. The Imperial City of the Mongol emperors measured no less than 6 miles in circumference. It contained the major government offices, the finest homes of the nobles and the palaces of the imperial family, which lined the lakes on the west.

Peking under the Ming and Qing

In 1368 the first Ming emperor changed the name of the city to Beiping fu (Peace of the North). But the Ming emperors made Nanking their first capital and did not move to Peking until 1409. Even then it was considered a temporary capital until 1450 and Nanking remained a phantom capital all through the Ming period. The Ming city (1419) was based on that of the Yuan, but 10 furlongs were lopped off on the north and 2½ added on the south. This gave it its present aspect – an almost square north section (the Imperial City of the Ming and Qing) and a rectangular section to the south (the Outer City).

The Walls

The approach to the city was dominated by the sturdy rhythm of lines and masses. Here for the first time brick was used for city walls. The ancient ramparts of rammed earth to the south, east and west were faced with brick and the new north wall was built entirely of that material. The wooden bridges over the moat were replaced by stone bridges. All the gates were reinforced with an outer tower for archers and an inner tower for drummers. This is how Father Ricci described the walls of Peking at the beginning of the seventeenth century: 'These walls are far higher than those we are used to in Europe. Soldiers always stand guard as if it was wartime and eunuchs are posted at the gates to collect duties.'

The perimeter of the ramparts was 14 miles 5 furlongs. Their height and thickness varied. The north wall was 39 feet high on the outside and 30 on the inside; it was about 54 feet thick at the top and 75 at the foot. The east wall (between the Donzhi men and the Qihua men) was about 36 feet high on the outside and 35 feet on the inside; it was 37 feet thick at the top and 55 at the foot. The brick facing too varied in thickness; at some points there were as many as seven or eight layers. They rested on a plinth of sandstone ashlars. The scarp varied also. For the north wall it was over 11 feet on a height of less than 33; elsewhere it ranged from 5 to 6 feet. There was a bastion every 220 yards on the north wall and every 90 yards or so on the others. The summit of the rampart was paved with large bricks and edged with a parapet on the inside and crenelated battlements on the outside. The parapet was about 2 feet thick and 3 feet high; the battlements three times as high. Square openings were cut in the wall for drainage.

Most of the vicissitudes in the history of Peking between the fifteenth century and the twentieth – war and peace, good times and bad – left their mark on the wall. In fact, today it does not present the same aspect along the entire perimeter. Besides the differences in size and general appearance, the successive restorations carried out from the end of the fifteenth century to the beginning of the twentieth are clear to see. Inscriptions with the date and extent of the repairs and the names of the officials responsible for them reveal technical differences in the masonry between the Ming and Qing periods.

In the sixteenth century there was a plan to build an outer wall enclosing the suburbs, but the project was too ambitious and all that was actually done was to join the west and east walls of the Outer City with the wall of the Imperial City in 1569.

The Gates

The whole life of the city flowed through the gates, which were shut at night. Those of the Imperial City – Europeans called it the 'Tartar City' – were sited as follows: three to the south, two to the north (which always played an important part in the defence of the city), two to the west and two to the east; one of the latter was the Dongzhi men, through which supplies of rice were brought in. The seven gates of the Outer City (the 'Chinese City' of the Europeans) were smaller but distributed in the same way.

The main feature of the gates of the Imperial City was the double tower that defended them. The inner tower, erected on the top of the wall, which was strengthened by a bastion at that point, had the shape of a large pavilion with a three-tiered roof and verandahs on the two main storeys. Its terrace was reached by ramps. The outer tower resembled a fortress; it was built of brick with sloping walls and two-tiered roof. Though their defences were inadequate after the introduction of fire arms, these gates were useful as customs barriers until the end of the nineteenth century. Many of the gates no longer display their original aspect; in many cases the outer tower has been destroyed and the inner tower rebuilt. For instance, the present Qian men, formerly Zhengyang men, in the south wall of the Imperial City is but a mutilated vestige of the splendid edifice that marked the main entrance to the political heart of the city. Originally there was a very large U-shaped courtyard with four openings at the four points of the compass. The north gate, under the great inner tower, faced the outer gate of the Palace (Daqing men). The south gate, under the outer tower, faced the south-north axis of the Outer City. Only the emperor used this gate; common mortals passed through the openings to the east and west. The courtyard was 118 yards long and 93 yards wide. The enclosing wall, 22 yards thick at the base, formed an excellent defence for the Imperial City.

The Republic commissioned a German architect named Rothkegel to study a new layout for the Qian men, and his project was put into effect in 1915–16. The surrounding wall was demolished and the court-yard became an open space with the outer tower at its southern end. The 125-foot tower itself was restored in a spirit that was quite alien to its original style.

The Blocks

Peking was built round a south-north axis that starts at the middle gate in the south wall of the Outer City and runs for 5 miles to the Drum and Bell Towers. As a rule the streets were not paved. Those in the residential blocks were about 84 yards apart, the intervening space being occupied by dwelling houses. The blocks were all oriented towards the four cardinal points and the houses concealed by walls of grey brick, often coated with a red wash, devoid of windows or other decoration. There was no guessing from the monotonous streets in the residential quarters of Peking the beauty of the homes sheltered behind those plain walls. The situation was reversed in the trading quarters (for instance, to the south of the Qian men), where the houses opened on to the street with lattice doors and windows.

Here is a vivid description by an eighteenth-century traveller: 'One is astonished to see the enormous crowds that fill these streets, where there is not a woman to be seen, and the jams caused by the amazing number of horses, mules, donkeys, camels, wagons and sedan chairs, not to mention the knots of one or two hundred men who gather in every open space to listen to fortune-tellers, thimble-riggers, ballad-singers and others who read or tell comic tales ... or sorts of quacks who are eloquent in extolling the miraculous properties of the remedies they distribute. Anyone not of the commonalty would be stopped repeatedly were he not preceded by a horseman who wards off the crowd and exhorts them to give way. This city is the goal of all the wealth and merchandise of the empire. One rides through the streets on horseback or in a sedan chair. The mule drivers know the streets perfectly and the houses where the most important persons live. One can even buy a book that gives information on the quarters, the squares, the streets and the homes of all public personages.' (J. B. du Halde, 1735.)

Besides the shops and markets, fairs were held periodically in certain quarters. For instance, outside the Chongwen men (Hada men) there was a flower market every 4th, 14th and 24th day of the month. The flowers were mostly made of paper for women to stick in their hair. There was also a pigeon market. The Liuli chang fair (outside the Chien men) was famous for the toys, jewelry and antiques sold there during the first fifteen days of the first month.

When the Ming dynasty came into power a system of brick drains was installed in the main portion of the city for discharging rainwater and sewage.

The Drum and Bell Towers

The oldest civil edifice still standing in Peking is probably the Drum Tower—a massive bastion in rammed earth faced with brick and pierced by two tunnels. The upper half is a two-storey structure surrounded by a verandah and topped by a two-tier roof. This monumental building may well be the Yuan Tower that was restored and partly renovated in 1420. The structural details are simpler and the proportions clumsier than in other edifices of the same type, for instance the gates of the Palace City, which date from the Ming and Qing dynasties.

The Bell Tower (1745) replaced an early fifteenth-century tower that stood a little to the west of the Yuan Tower. It stands on a lofty square brick platform pierced by two corridors that intersect in the centre and has two storeys, the second of which is also pierced by a vaulted passage.

Tentative Conclusions

It is too early to draw conclusions as to the evolution of town planning in China. Too many details are still lacking, particularly as regards the merchant classes and the status of artisans at different periods. Men of letters have left little information on urban activities not connected with administration or culture. In this respect they echo official opinion and the government's contempt for trade. Provincial chronicles, which might offer a better idea of the development of the smaller towns and enable them to be included in

a general study of urbanism, have been largely neglected hitherto. Evolution seems to have slowed down after the Song. In Kaifeng we can glimpse a trend towards the bursting of the closed social cells, the liberation of trade, and a more extensive symbiosis of the various elements of the urban population. This is still clearer in Hangzhou.

Under the Ming, instead, the blocks were closed again, supervision became stricter, fortifications were the major public works, artisans and tradesmen were allowed less liberty. From the fourteenth century on the trading cities of the Song vegetated but did not develop. Life within the walls was regulated by those two pillars of law and order—hierarchy and etiquette. Urban architecture came more and more to symbolize the sovereignty of an emperor who lived secluded in his palace. (It would be interesting to study the very important part played by the eunuchs in the police and the civic administration.) These features became more marked under the Qing, who did little more than restore existing buildings and embellish the imperial residences. The modernity of the Song cities seems to have languished inside the walls of Peking just as under the Ming permissiveness was replaced by an official rigorism that increased steadily until the nineteenth century. When the Europeans appeared on the scene the closed cities of the interior were neglected and both population and economic activity were concentrated in the coastal cities like Shanghai and Canton, where life centred round the foreign concessions, the budding industries and the intellectual contributions of the Occidentals. For this reason they were at once in China and outside China.

Public Works—The Great Wall

During the epoch of the Warring States, those in Northern China built long stretches of ramparts for defence against barbarian raids. These ramparts of earth and rubble reinforced in some places by blocks of stone were joined together by Qin Shi huang di to form a single wall in order to withstand attacks by the Xiongnu. Manpower was provided by a vast army of convicts. From the Han to the Sui the wall was kept in good repair and new sections were added. Under Wen di, founder of the Sui dynasty, 30,000 men were employed to rebuild or restore it in 585 and 150,000 were engaged the following year. Under Yang di 1 million men were sent to the northern marches in 607 and 200,000 in 608. From the sixth century to the fourteenth this line of cleavage between China and the barbarian world lost its strategic importance. But when the Ming repulsed the Mongols their first concern was to rebuild the wall to ward off further invasion. The new rampart, which was begun in 1368, finished about 1500 and restored in the sixteenth century, rose to the south of the previous one. It extended almost 1700 miles, from the River Yalu in the east to the Jiayu guan pass in Gansu.

The layout varies greatly from one section to the next, depending on the terrain – the lowest point lies 8 feet below sea level, the highest 10,000 feet above – the materials available and subsequent restorations. The eastern section, some 30 miles north of Peking, is a splendid example of Ming architecture and is closely akin to the finest city walls in Northern China. It averages from 20 to 26 feet in height and is faced with ashlar. The top is paved with several courses of brick very precisely bonded to prevent water infiltrating. The sides show a very marked slope, the thickness being 21 feet 4 inches at the base and 19 feet at the summit. This latter is typical of the rammed earth walls of North-West China and serves to strengthen them. The crenelated battlements on the outer face are almost 5 feet high. Arched gates, approach ramps and watchtowers are arranged at intervals. The latter, which rise 12 or 13 feet above the rampart proper, numbered 20,000 during the Ming period. The main gates, which are located at points of difficult access were strongly fortified. At the most important strategic positions there were as many as nine walls one behind the other.

No other country has even imagined, much less realized, a project at once so vast and of such defensive value. This aspect of the Great Wall as a fortification often leads one to overlook the part it played as a means of communication. It formed a highway which along much of its length was broad enough for five horses to walk abreast.

Bridges

The development of bridge building in China was closely linked with the geographical characteristics of the country. Suspension bridges spanned the torrents in the mountain regions; flat stone bridges made wheeled transport easy in Northern China; arch bridges let river craft pass in the south. This development was also linked with the importance of the ancient carriage roads in Northern China, which were as straight as those the Romans built, and with the huge engineering works required to cope with the threat of the Yellow River in the north, the Min in the west and the Yanzi in the centre, to mention but three of the most important.

Chinese bridges may be divided into five types: floating bridges (made of pontoons or rafts lashed together with ropes) for temporary or seasonal use; suspension bridges with cables made of rope, bamboo fibre or iron (from the sixth century on); girder, cantilever and arch bridges.

Girder Bridges

This seems to have been the type of bridge most in use under the Han. Stamped bricks show that many bridges of the period had a 45-degree slope at each end. But they were seldom high enough to let large boats pass and their piers, too, hampered navigation. A certain number of bridges of this type were built in Fujian under the Song on a scale unheard-of in the rest of the world. The most famous is the Luoyang qiao at Quanzhou – Marco Polo's Zayton – which was a centre of foreign trade in full development during the thirteenth century. This bridge was built between 1053 and 1059; its piers are made of great blocks of granite placed one above the other and its beams well deserve to be termed megaliths. An islet divides the bridge into two parts; the north section has forty-one piers, the south section seven. The total length is 590 yards and each of the forty-seven spans comprises seven beams 12 yards long and 16 to 20 inches broad. The vicinity of the sea and the high tides made the erection of this bridge an extremely difficult task.

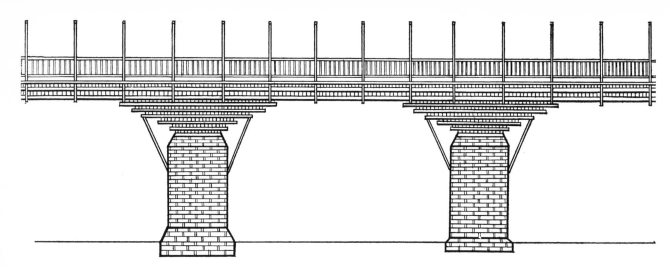

Part of the cantilever bridge at Lilin, Hunan, from Willetts, 'Chinese Art'

Cantilever Bridges in Timber and Stone

A deck of transverse planks rests as a rule on the timber girders that form the framework of the bridge; a horizontal parapet runs along each side supported at regular intervals by vertical posts. The piers may be of masonry, as in the famous bridge at Lilin, Hunan. There the five tiers of the cantilever beaming are strengthened by two slanting beams that link the fourth tier to the masonry pier. Some bridges of this type have a single central girder supported by a system of brackets at both ends. In this case the abutments are corbelled and support the deck.

Arch Bridges

The culmination of bridge building in China was the cradle vault – usually semicircular, sometimes two-centred, more seldom segmental. The arches of the vault may be arranged in three different ways.
1. In the first, each curved row of voussoirs is built separately; there is no link between the various arches that form the vault. This method, which was

Variants in the arrangement of arch stones

a Each row of voussoirs is laid separately
b The voussoirs are laid in courses of the same height from the springer to the keystone
c Binders are inserted between the courses

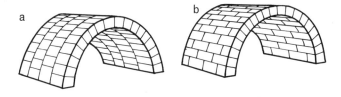

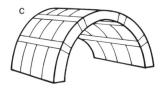

used for the Zhaoxian bridge, has the advantage that if one part gives way the entire structure does not collapse; it also makes repairs easier. Its drawback is the absence of a bond between the arches.

2. The vault is made of courses of the same height from the springer to the keystone.

3. Between the courses a header traverses the vault in depth, linking the various rows of curved voussoirs. This third method, which was employed chiefly under the Ming and Qing, combines the convenience of the first with the solidity of the second.

The oldest arch bridge still standing is the Anji qiao at Zhaoxian in Hebei. Erected under the Sui by Li Chun between 606 and 618, it was the first big flat arch bridge not only in China but in the whole world. The design is absolutely modern: a single flat arch with a span of 123 feet and a rise of less than 4 feet. At each end are two small spandrel arches whose function is to lighten the structure and reduce the load on the main arch beside providing spillways for floodwater. Maximum width is 31 feet 6 inches (30 feet 2 inches in the middle). The roadway is bordered by a carved stone balustrade.

This bridge had a very great influence on the development of arch bridge building during the Sui and Tang periods. It is clear to see in the Jimei bridge, also at Zhaoxian, which has five arches (three smaller

A rainbow-arch bridge at Kaifeng under the Northern Song, from the 'Qing ming shang he tu' scroll

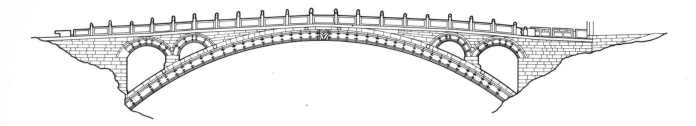

The Anji qiao, an arch bridge at Zhaoxian (Hebei) built between 606 and 618

and two larger). The Anji qiao was built at a time when immense public works were undertaken to improve communications in the reunited empire; it was perfectly suited to conditions in Northern China, a flat region where most transport was by road.

Other famous bridges still standing are the Baodai qiao south-west of Suzhou (Jiangsu), over 100 yards long with 53 arches, and the Lugui qiao south-west of Peking, which Europeans call the Marco Polo Bridge. Built by the Jin between 1189 and 1192, it is 257 yards long and almost 9 yards wide. Its eleven arches vary in span from 52 feet 5 inches at the ends to 70 feet 10 inches in the middle. On each side there is a balustrade with 140 little columns each supporting a marble lion. The bridge was restored under the Ming in 1444 and again in 1698. This is how Marco Polo, who visited Khanbalic (Peking) in the thirteenth century, described it: 'On this river is a very handsome stone bridge: few indeed are as handsome. It is a good 300 paces long and eight broad, for ten horsemen can easily ride abreast. . . . It is all in light-brown marble, very well and solidly built. At each side of the bridge there is a wall of marble slabs and columns made as follows: At the head of the bridge there is a marble column supported by a marble lion and at the top of the column another marble lion; these lions are very handsome, big and cleverly carved. A pace beyond this column is another identical one. . . .'

Bridges whose timber framework forms an unsupported arch count among the finest Chinese achievements in this field. They are often called 'rainbow bridges' and under the Northern Song the capital Kaifeng could boast three. One, situated seven li outside the Dongshui Gate, is depicted in a famous scroll in the Peking Imperial Museum entitled 'By the River at the Qing ming Festival' (Qing ming shang he tu). The arch, which has a span of about 22 yards is formed by a series of five arch-beams, each supported by two cross-beams that rest in turn on two other arch-beams. Segmental arch bridges of this type consist of two systems of arch-beams whose ends rest on cross-beams. These latter, which support one system of arch-beams, rest in turn on the arch-beams of the next system; they perform the dual function of ties and supports, besides serving to distribute the load.

Plates

Peking: the Forbidden City

1 Courtyard between the Taihe men and the terrace that supports the three great ceremonial halls (Taihe dian, Zhonghe dian and Baohe dian) of the official part of the Imperial Palace.

2- The Imperial Palace: the three entrance gates and
3 the courtyard before the Taihe dian terrace. Note the double, half-hipped roof of the Taihe men.

4 The Taihe dian (Pavilion of Supreme Harmony) on the three-tier, white marble terrace that supports the three big pavilions on the south-north axis.

5 The stairways to the Zhonghe dian (Pavilion of Middle Harmony); left, the Baohe dian (Pavilion of Protecting Harmony), the last of the three big pavilions of the official part of the Palace.

6- Marble stairways and balustrades of the three-tier
7 terrace in the official part of the Imperial Palace.

68 Imperial Palace, Peking: official part, stairway to the Zhonghe dian.

69 Detail of white marble terrace of the Imperial Palace.

70 Roofs of pavilions of the Imperial Palace; 'chiwei' at the ends of the ridge beam and 'kuilongzi', human and animal silhouettes, aligned on the arris of the half-hipped roof, stand out against the sky.

71 A succession of courtyards and galleries in the private part of the Imperial Palace.

72 Imperial Palace, Peking, official part: the River of Golden Water (Jinshui he) in the courtyard between the Wu men and Taihe men. In the foreground, balustrade of one of the five bridges.

73 The River of Golden Water in the Imperial Palace.

74 A covered way in the Forbidden City. The paintings on the ceiling are good examples of Qing decoration.

75 Courtyard surrounded by pavilions in the private part of the Palace.

76 The south façade of the Wu men, southern entrance to the Palace, with a corner of the west wing.

77 Doors of the Palace of Peace and Long Life in the north-east corner of the Imperial Palace.

Peking: the Temple of Heaven

78 General view of the Temple of Heaven, Peking. From south to north on the median axis lie the Altar of Heaven, the Huangqiongyu and the Qinian dian.

79 The Qinian dian (Hall for Prayers for an Abundant Harvest), on its three white marble terraces in the centre of a square courtyard that is entered from the south. Behind the Qinian dian, on a lower level, stands the Huangqian dian.

80 The Qinian dian with the stairway that gives access from the south. The hall, which was built to a circular plan in 1420 is almost 100 feet in diameter. The three rows of pillars that support the triple roof symbolize the twelve months of the year, the twelve hours of the day and the four seasons.

81 The Temple of Heaven, Peking: the gatehouse, like all the temple buildings, is covered with glazed blue tiles.

82 Each of the two enclosures (one circular, one square) that surround the Altar of Heaven has three white marble portals at each cardinal point. Here we see those to the north facing the Huangqiongyu. In the background, the roof of the Qinian dian. In the foreground, terraces of the Altar of Heaven.

83 Portals of the enclosures that surround the Altar of Heaven. Like the 'pailou' that offer access to the Imperial Tombs, these portals have uprights crowned by wing-like appendages embellished with cloud motifs.

84 The Huangqiongyu of the Temple of Heaven. This small building, erected in 1530 on the white marble terrace, is 64 feet high and 51 feet in diameter.

◀ Plans

Notes

The Treatise on Architecture by Li Mingzhong

From the earliest times Chinese architecture has been subject to official regulation and officials have been entrusted with the direction of building operations. For that task they could refer to documents and records. Unfortunately we know very little about the regulations prior to the Song period, which were replaced by the 'Ying zao fa shi', written in the twelfth century. That work and fragments of the 'Mu jing', an early Song treatise on carpentry by Yu Hao at the beginning of the Song period, are our major sources of information on the architecture of that time.

The 'Ying zao fa shi' of Li Mingzhong

The author Li Jie (called Mingzhong), who came from Zhengzhou (Henan), was all his life long a subordinate official and ended his career as assistant inspector at the Department of Public Works. He was apparently a gifted calligrapher, painter and bibliophile. But his chief claim to fame rests on the 'Ying zao fa shi', which he presented to the emperor in 1100. This compendium of Chinese architectural tradition and building methods in thirty-four chapters was published in 1103, seven years before the author's death.

After two chapters devoted to technical terms, the main part of the work (Chapters 3–15) contains rules concerning building methods, decoration, fabrication, the relative measurements and proportions of the various architectural elements. There are separate sections on:
– regulations concerning drains, palings, foundations and walls;
– regulations concerning stone working (Ch. 3);
– regulations concerning timber constructions, i.e. the framework (Ch. 4, 5);
– regulations concerning minor timber structures, i.e. doors, windows, partitions, staircases (Ch. 6–11);
– regulations concerning wood sculpture and engraving (Ch. 12);
– regulations concerning roofing in pottery, tiles, mortar, and furnace building (Ch. 13);
– regulations concerning painted decoration (Ch. 14), brickwork and glazed tiles (Ch. 15).

Chapters 16–28 deal with working norms and job classification. Work was not paid for on a time basis but on a job basis. Thus 60 lbs of dry earth made up a 'load' and carrying a 'load' a given distance and back made up a 'job'. Some operations were defined by the number of 'jobs' they involved. This was done to facilitate organization. Chapters 29–34 contain illustrations.

The Historical Value of the 'Ying zao fa shi'

The plates and virtually all the copies of the first edition of the 'Ying zao fa shi' (1103) disappeared when Kaifeng was sacked in 1126. In 1145, under the Song, a second edition was printed at Suzhou but no copy has survived. A transcribed version copied in 1821 was reproduced in 1920 (Commercial Press, Shanghai). A folio and a half presumed to be part of the 1103 edition was discovered in the National Library, Peking, in 1918 and was published in 1925.

To make use of this work is no easy matter. The difficult text has never been translated and some of the illustrations are not entirely reliable. The designs of the decorative motifs seem to have been altered by successive copyists who could not help interpreting the originals in accordance with the taste of their own time.

It served, however, as a model for such later works as the 'Gong cheng zuo fa li' published in 1734, and its instructions for carpenters, masons and decorators give us an idea of the position and importance of the architect in twelfth-century China. His main task was to tackle tough technical problems.

Was he nothing more than a master builder experienced in the work of selecting, calculating and utilizing materials, capable of supervising the erection of an edifice in its every slightest detail? It is too soon to answer that question, for as yet no one has made a synthetic study of architects' biographies or of their exact part in the evolution of official architecture.

64

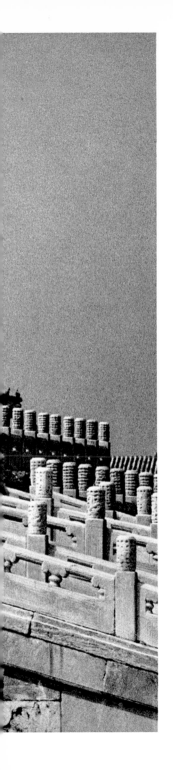

79

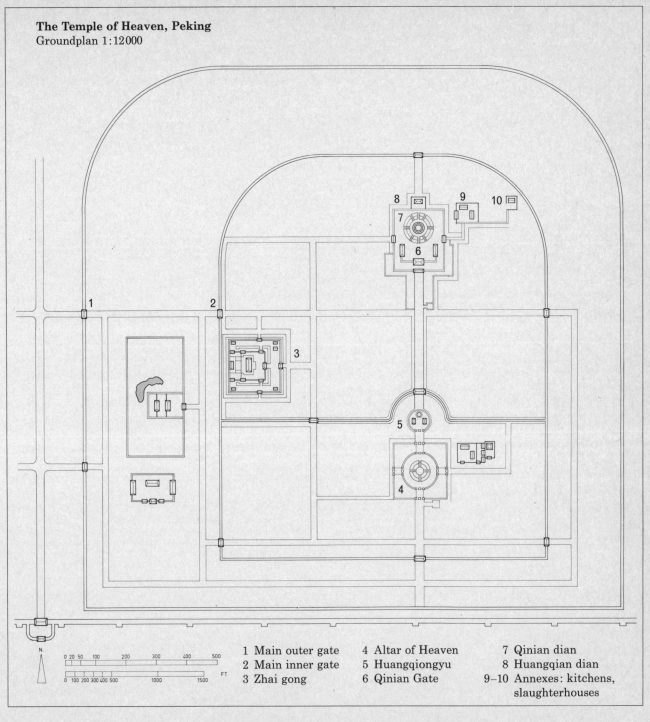

The Temple of Heaven, Peking
Groundplan 1:12000

N.

0 20 50 100 200 300 400 500
0 100 200 300 400 500 1000 1500
FT

1 Main outer gate
2 Main inner gate
3 Zhai gong

4 Altar of Heaven
5 Huangqiongyu
6 Qinian Gate

7 Qinian dian
8 Huangqian dian
9–10 Annexes: kitchens,
    slaughterhouses

The Temple of Guanyin (Dule si), Jixian (Hebei)
Cross-section 1:150. Built in 984

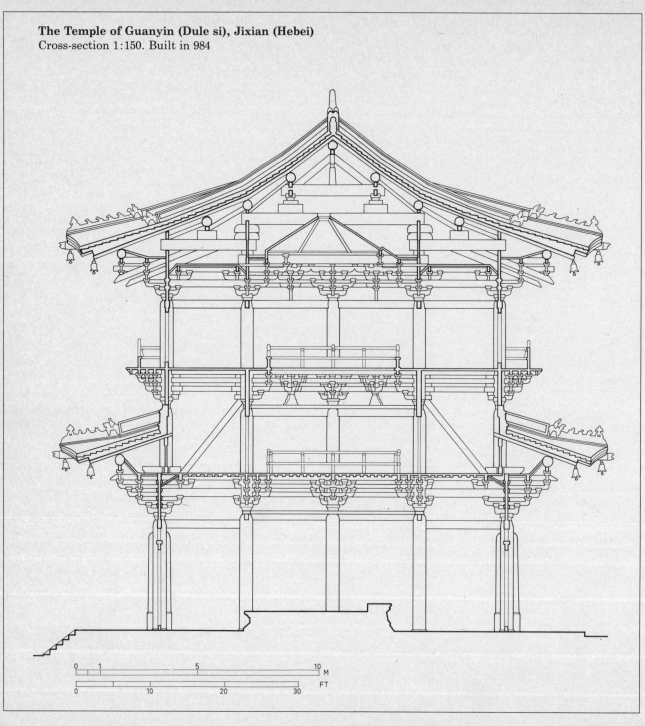

3. Imperial Palaces and Temples

In China the Imperial Palace was always a city within the capital. The emperor lived there as a rule out of touch with the rest of the world, surrounded by women, eunuchs and the few courtiers who had access to him outside council meetings and official ceremonies.

Before describing some of those palaces, I think it a good idea to specify the various elements that make up a Chinese edifice and set forth its major structural features. We shall see later that these notions are valid for palaces, temples and private houses.

The Various Parts of the Building
1. The Terrace and Its Balustrades

In China every large building stands on a terrace faced with brick or stone. The custom of always building on a podium derives perhaps from the need to protect timber structures from the weather. It goes back at least to the Shang period, when the largest terraces in rammed earth measured over 1200 square yards. During the Warring States epoch there were over twenty large platforms in the city of Yanxia (Hebei) alone, the largest of which had a surface of over 18,000 square yards and were 66 feet high. These platforms were originally stepped and each step supported timber structures.

The terraces of the palaces still extant in Northern China date mostly from the Ming or Qing periods. The most impressive are to be found in the imperial ensemble in Peking – the Forbidden City, the Temple of Heaven and the Ming Tombs. They are faced with white marble, which forms a striking contrast with the multi-coloured timber buildings they support.

Access to the terraces is usually by ramp or stairway, whose long slanting lines stress the horizontality of the terraces themselves. Stairways and terraces are bordered by balustrades, which are of white marble in Peking but may also be of brick or wood. The most usual type of stone balustrade has sturdy little columns slightly higher than the handrail; the square or hexagonal shaft is crowned by a sculptured ornament, mostly a lion seated on a lotus flower. The spaces between the columns are filled with decorated panels. Wooden balustrades are also divided into

Reconstruction of a Shang house at Anyang (fourteenth to eleventh centuries B.C.) showing the platform with pillars supporting the roof, from Shih Chang-ju, Annals, Academica Sinica No. 1 (1954)

panels with ornamental fretted patterns that owe their effect to the rhythmic, symmetric repetition of simple motifs.

2. Pillars

The supporting members of a building are not walls but pillars. The area of the building is measured in bays, a bay being the space delimited by four pillars. These latter may be of stone or timber, round (smooth or fluted), octagonal, square, sculptured with dragon motifs, or quatrefoil. Their base is usually of stone but sometimes of wood. During the Shang period these bases were flat stones or bronze discs; later their shape ranged from plain drum, square and octagon to ornate lotus-petal carving.

a) Proportions

Thick and sturdy under the Tang, these pillars became tall and slender under the Ming and Qing. The impression of stability Tang buildings give is due not only to the diameter of the piers but also to the fact that their height and interval forms a square space. Besides which, the height of the inner and outer pillars is the same. During the Tang and early Liao periods the ratio of height to diameter ranged from 8:1 to 9:1. Under the Song and Jin the outer pillars kept these sturdy proportions, while the inner pillars became taller and more slender and their height increased from the middle of the hall towards the two sides – a feature seldom found after the fourteenth century. From the Yuan period on the ratio of height to diameter varied between 9:1 and 11:1. To increase the diameter Song builders employed pillars made of two, three or four pieces. Under the Qing slim pillars were faced with thick planks for the same purpose.

b) Inclination

In China pillars are never vertical: they always slant towards the inside of the building. This inclination may be as great as 2.9 per cent of the height but becomes very slight from the fifteenth century on.

c) Arrangement

A building cannot have fewer than four pillars – one at each corner. Many large halls have two rows of pillars that divide the area into three naves. There is often an additional colonnade outside, forming an open portico on the front, if not all round, and joined to the wall piers by cross-beams. Since the depth of a hall depends on the length of the beams that support the roof, Chinese buildings are usually long and shallow; greater depth could be obtained by multiplying the longitudinal colonnades. A new method of augmenting the useful space appeared towards the middle of the Liao period, developed under the Jin and Yuan but disappeared again under the Ming and Qing except for small buildings. It consisted in reducing the number of inner pillars and was employed, for instance, in the Wenshu pavilion of the Foguang si on Mount Wutai, built in 1137.

Instead of a capital, Chinese pillars have a cluster of cantilever brackets that radiate, in principle, towards the four cardinal points and support the beams. These latter may be mortised into the pillars or pass right through them.

3. The Structural Framework

The structural framework with its timber beams and pillars is perhaps the most original feature of Chinese architecture. It is already found fully developed under the Han dynasty. The various elements are joined by tenon and mortise and have always been so from the Warring States epoch. In course of time the beams grew thicker and thicker. Under the Tang the diameter/length ratio was 1:2, under the Song it was 2:3; and the process continued until under the Qing it reached 4:5 or even 5:6. Under the Yuan the extremely thick beams were often made by attaching two pieces of the same length. Later, under the Qing, beams were faced in the same way as pillars.

By and large, Chinese architecture always tended to maintain the frame system of the rectangular pavilion, even in circular and polygonal buildings. The perimeter and roof may be circular, as in the Dazhong si, north of Peking, but the structure is always based on a square.

The various elements of the framework were joined, from the Tang and Qing periods on, either by brackets or by tuofeng, which are ornamental wooden blocks that serve to distribute the load evenly on the beam. This member, which first appears in the Buddhist rock-cut shrines of the Six Dynasties period in the shape of an inverted V, developed under the Tang

Construction of stepped roof truss in traditional Chinese building, after Willetts, 'Chinese Art'

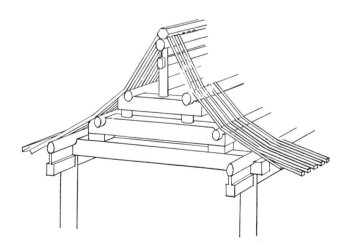

dynasty (for instance on the lintel of the Dayan ta) into a curving motif whose function was almost purely decorative.

a) The Roof Truss

In the Chinese structural framework the length of the beams decreases progressively as the building grows higher. Each main beam supports a pair of queen posts on which rests another, shorter beam. The purlins that support the rafters rest on the queen posts and beam ends of each tier.

Where the assemblage that forms the roof truss is concerned, Chinese methods differ entirely from those of the west. In the triangular western truss the struts bear the weight of the purlins on which the rafters that carrying the roofing are fixed; the sole function of the tie-beam is to maintain the struts at the proper distance but it must have considerable tensile strength for it subtends the load-bearing members. Consequently, the western roof truss has the form of a rigid triangle whose base is the tie-beam and whose two sides are the two slanting struts, which stretch from the eaves to the ridge pole. The sides of the triangle are straight and the typical roof, viewed in profile, has the shape of an inverted V.

The Chinese roof truss is a far more complex system. The main beam supports, through the intermediary of the queen posts and shorter upper beams, all or part of the weight of the roof. Thus the roof truss rises in steps until the required height is attained. Very often there are no struts and the purlins are supported by queen posts fixed vertically in the beams. This system has the immense advantage that it enables the roof to be given a concave or convex curve at will.

b) The Ceiling

Most Tang and Song buildings had a ceiling and the timbers above it were left rough; but the lower, visible beams were carefully finished. Where there was no ceiling all the timbers were accurately squared. This custom spread under the Ming and Qing to all buildings, whether they had a ceiling or not.

Ceilings were flat, with a single coffer – this form was used for the centre of large halls in temples and palaces – or with complex coffers that could be circular, square or octagonal. This third form, which was termed zaojing (literally, 'aquatic plants tank'), is documented in palaces and tombs from the beginning of our era, and owed its name to the patterns of water plants that adorned the panels of the ceiling. Those plants were visualized as hanging down and the image was that of a tank full of plants viewed upside down. The motif was intended to avert the risk of fire.

The coffers were formed by a series of superposed elements – a rectangle constituted by the framework of the ceiling, an octagon inscribed in a square, or a shape with eight projecting and eight re-entrant angles in two superposed squares. Under the Qing dynasty the ornate ceilings above the throne in the major edifices of the Imperial Palace in Peking were often embellished at the summit of the intrados by a sculptured dragon from whose mouth dangled a ball at the end of a wire.

4. The Roof

The great development of the roof in Chinese buildings was due to the fact that the entrance was not located under a gable but in the middle of a long side. To make this vast roof seem less ponderous Chinese architects preferred to give it a broken line or, later, to give the eaves an upward tilt that made the roof look as if suspended at the four corners.

a) Roof Forms

The beam frame system adopted in China made it possible to give the roof a great variety of shapes. And since in that country climatic conditions and regional traditions vary enormously, the potential variants were virtually unlimited – from the flat roof to the hip roof via the pent roof, the round roof, the gable and the half-hip. In large pavilions the roof is often split into two tiers, the lower tier being much broader than the upper. This double roof arrangement breaks up and lightens the large masses, besides dividing and distributing the weight.

The gabled roof is typical of regional domestic architecture; so are flat, pent and round roofs. The fully hipped roof was used for important buildings, whether official, religious or private. It is the most impressive and harmonious of all Chinese roof forms. The half-hipped roof, which appeared under the Tang, or perhaps even earlier, is a combination of hip roof and gabled roof. It was much in use and is characterized by gables that end half-way up, where the roof starts to slope again.

Under the Ming and Qing the rank of a building was reflected in its roof. The noblest had a hipped double roof. This was followed by the half-hipped double roof, the simple hipped roof, the simple half-hipped roof and, lastly, the gabled roof.

The trend was from slightly sloping roofs under the Tang (one-sixth of the depth of the hall) towards taller, steeper roofs. The pitch ranged from a quarter to a third from the Song to the Ming and remained steady at a third under the Qing.

b) The Curve of the Roof

The curve of the eaves was the most original feature of Chinese roof design. The roof appears to have broken free from the supporting members, for the further it spreads beyond the building the more it seems to float above the colonnades. It crowns the edifice rather than covers it.

Under the Han dynasty roofs did not curve but they often had a sort of break half-way up, where the change of pitch gave the impression of a small double roof. In very deep halls it may have served the purpose of avoiding the exaggerated height of a rectilinear roof. The problem is very like that of the curved roof, which is obtained, if necessary, by assembling at obtuse angles at the ends of the rafters the requisite number of furrings.

The true curved roof seems to have developed at the beginning of the Tang period in Southern China, where it occurs in some tenth-century pagodas. In all probability it was not used in Northern China until the Song dynasty and may have been introduced in their capital by the architect Yu Hao, who came from Hangzhou. The origin of the curved roof, though laid

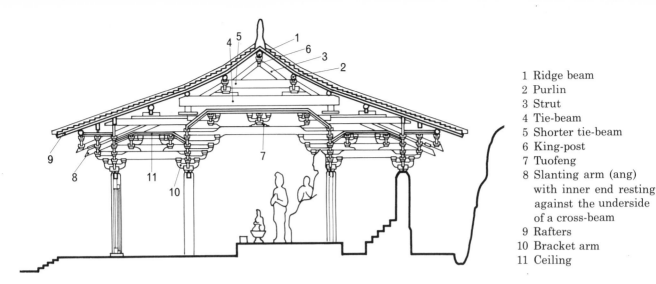

1 Ridge beam
2 Purlin
3 Strut
4 Tie-beam
5 Shorter tie-beam
6 King-post
7 Tuofeng
8 Slanting arm (ang)
  with inner end resting
  against the underside
  of a cross-beam
9 Rafters
10 Bracket arm
11 Ceiling

Framework, roof truss and bracket system of the main hall
of the Foguang si on Mount Wutai (Shanxi) built between
850 and 860

down as an axiom in 'Ying zao fa shi', the official
treatise on Song architecture written in 1100, is still
a moot question. W. Willetts (Chinese Art, Vol. II,
London 1958) suggests that at a certain moment the
curve became a natural element inherent in the structure of the roof. It may, he says, have derived from the
sag caused by the dead weight of the roofing materials
(notably the split bamboo lengths that served as tiles).
Then the inner supporting members may have been
designed to maintain the natural curve and a type of
construction evolved comprising horizontal beams
and vertical posts whose height could be adjusted to
suit the outer curve that the architect wanted to obtain. This hypothesis, though alluring in some re-
spects, is not altogether convincing and the answer
will not be found until studies on the inner evolution
of the roof elements have been completed together
with a more thorough collation of pre-Tang texts and
researches on alien influences. It is worth noting that
the development of the curved roof under the Song
went hand in hand with an increase in pitch and, in
the aesthetic field, with a deliberate pursuit of lightness.

c) The Roof Covering

In China, as in the west, the roof covering included
battens that rested on the rafters and supported the
tiles, but never directly. Between the battens and the
covering proper there was always at least one layer
of clay or very thin shingles.

The tiles were laid in rows from the ridge to the tip
of the eaves with the concave face up, thus forming
vertical gutters. To prevent water from filtering
through, the joint between two rows of tiles was covered by a third row with the convex face up. These
tiles were only slightly burnt and of a greyish colour
for ordinary buildings; for important edifices they
were glazed blue, yellow or green. Glazed tiles were
seemingly first imported from the west in the fifth
century. From then on they were manufactured at
Datong in Shânxi, which is still the major manufac-
turing centre. Tile shapes do not seem to have varied
greatly until the Song period and the major development took place under the Yuan. At that time four
kilns in the hills to the west worked for the Peking
palace. Their output was despatched by water to

Liulichang (now the antiquaries' quarter of Peking), where they were given a final polish.

During the Warring States epoch roofs were edged with round tiles and models of houses in pottery dating from about the beginning of our era already display highly ornate ridge pieces. It must have been at that time that the custom of placing ornamental motifs at the roof ends became widespread. One was a sort of dolphin with brandished tail, called 'owl's tail' ('chiwei'), which, like the tanks of aquatic plants painted on ceilings, was meant to avert fire. The twelfth-century 'Ying zao fa shi' mentions nine different animals atop the roof ridge. They prefigured the human and animal silhouettes called 'kuilongzi' aligned on the ridge poles of Ming and Qing buildings.

d) The Eave Brackets

The overhanging eaves typical of Chinese architecture served to drain off rainwater and to provide shade during the hot season. Since the roof was very massive, the eaves had to be supported by brackets. These brackets developed in the course of time into such elaborate systems, with so many subtle variants, that only the main outlines of the question can be touched on here. The term 'bracket system' (dougong) covers the aspect, arrangement and static function of all the members that help to support the eaves and the adjacent portions of the structure. The 'bracket arm' is the basic component of the system and its main function is to provide an independent point of support at its tip. Lastly, the term 'bracket cluster' (buzuo) designates a group of bracket arms with their accessory members all springing from a single point of support. The effective horizontal reach of a bracket arm is called a step, while its useful vertical height is a tier. Consequently, one may speak of a two-step, three-tier cluster, indicating one that extends outwards in two stages and carries its load upwards through three (e.g. on the lintel of the Dayan ta at Sian). The bracket, which is the typical unit of the system, is a combination of three members – at the base a supporting block on which rests a long arm that carries three small blocks at equal intervals for sustaining the purlins.

The inscriptions on some ancient bronzes seem to indicate that this system first appeared at the end of the Warring States epoch. Under the Han the brackets were not incorporated in the structural framework but formed separate supports. The bracket cluster never had more than one step nor rose higher than two tiers. It was not until the Tang period that the system attained its full development and complexity. During that period the increasing spread of the eaves led perforce to a greater number of steps and tiers. The brackets became the active part of the structure. Some, like those of the main hall of the Foguang si on Mount Wutai, are over two feet wide. On the lintel of the Dayan ta at Sian (eighth century) the combinations of lengthways and transverse brackets seem to be standardized.

At that time the eaves were supported solely on the axes of the pillars and the system gives an impression of great clarity. The Song period was marked by two innovations in this field. The eaves were supported between the pillars, too, and a slanting arm was introduced whose inner end provided a direct support for the eaves' purlin.

The first of these innovations appears in the Goguang si (857). The bracket clusters on and between the pillars are not yet identical and the intermediate brackets are still simple in form, but support the purlin and therefore constitute a decisive advance on the Tang system. These brackets were repeated under the Song; under the Ming and Qing they were multiplied to the point where they formed a continuous ornamental cornice. At this point decoration overshadowed the rigorously functional yet ingenious use of timber that had been the major feature of Ming and Song architecture, where each member served a precise purpose. The Ming and Qing brackets were small and non-functional. In the Imperial Palace in Peking they form a simple frieze under the roof and the purlins rest on jutting beams.

The Slanting Bracket Arm

The roof was supported not only by bracket clusters but also by lever action. The slanting arm (ang) first appeared about the third century A.D. and always

...d one of the most effective members of the
... It was placed directly under the roof and ex-
...d parallel to the rafters, ending under the outer-
...urlin, which it supported by means of a bracket
...ss-beam. Its rake contrasts with the horizontal
...rtical lines of the structure and adds a dynamic
...the whole system.

...he Song period the inner end of the slanting
...ted simply on the underside of a beam; this

required a ceiling on the sides of a hall to mask it. Researches under the Song dynasty led to an improved and more effective design of the ang. The slanting timber was left in full view and served as a true lever arm to balance the inner and outer load. The decorative effect of its vivid, active line was linked with its structural function. An example of this can be seen in the Chuzu an of the Shaolin si (Song shan, Henan).

The slanting arm may be twinned for greater strength. Later a horizontal member ending in a sharp point and called sham ang simulated a second slanting arm underneath the real one. This sham ang, which was added to the real ang under the Yuan dynasty, spread under the Ming and was in general use under the Qing. At that time the eaves were supported by an additional row of pillars directly under the maximum overhang, which did away with the need for points of support in the plane of the wall. The slanting arm lost its practical function and, like the bracket cluster, became a mere ornament. Compared with the flexible, dynamic structural system of the Tang and Song, the monotonous new procedure represented a sort of sclerosis.

The Palaces
The Palaces of the Early Periods

A palace is a group of separate buildings enclosed by a wall. The ancient Chinese palaces were built of perishable materials and all that remains today are the terraces on which they stood. Palace sites have been discovered in the Shang capitals of Zhengzhou and Anyang in Henan, and in the cities of the Warring States (Linzi in Shandong, Handan and Xiadu in Hebei). A mound some 40 feet high is the only vestige of the Afang palace Qin Shi huang di erected at Xiangyang (by the River Wei, west of the present-day Sian).

Some fifty palaces have been located at Anyang. Most of them were rectangular or U-shaped and rested on rammed-earth foundations that supported the stone bases of the timber pillars. The general layout of these vestiges seems to show that the arrangement of the buildings round a courtyard with a south-north axis first appeared at that period.

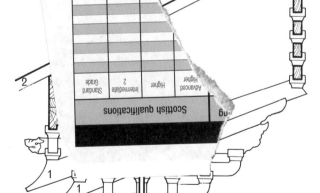

...ter (buzuo) and lever arm (ang) of the Shanhua
s... (Shanxi), Liao dynasty (eleventh century)

1 ...ng)
2 ...
3 S...
4 Br...
5 Bea... ...hrough the tops of the pillars longitudinal...
6 Be... ...ugh the tops of the pillars transversely
(... ...he Liao dynasty on

Recent excavations of the sites of the end of the Zhou dynasty bear witness to a certain evolution. The royal palaces became steadily larger from the sixth to the third century B.C.

Linzi (sixth-fifth centuries)	area	82×72 yards
Handan (early fourth century)	area	330×220 yards
Xiadu (fourth century)	area	140×150 yards
Afang gong (third century)	area	1300×500 yards

The Han Period

The Weiyang Palace in Changan, capital of the Western Han and built in 199 B.C., stood on a hillock in the south-west section of the city. Its enclosure comprised several buildings of which not a trace remains. The great historian Sima Qian tells how Gao Zu, the first Han emperor (206–194 B.C.), took possession of his new palace: 'The grand counsellor Xiao He had built the Weiyang Palace to his own plans; he had raised an east gate, a north gate, a front hall, an arms depot, a granary. When he returned, Gao Zu found that the proportions of palace and gates were exaggerated. He flew into a rage and said to Xiao He: "The empire resounds with wailing; it has suffered war for many years; there is no certainty of victory or defeat. Why build palaces that exceed all bounds?" Xiao He replied: "It is just because the empire has not yet recovered tranquillity that palaces can be erected at the present time; besides, the Son of Heaven has the whole country bounded by the four seas for his home. What can augment his prestige, if not the size and beauty (of his edifices)?" Gao Zu was satisfied.' (Les Mémoires Historiques, Vol. II, p. 391.) This text is symptomatic of a policy in which the style and luxury of a palace is an instrument of prestige, a symbol of the virtues of the imperial government. It was a policy adopted by all the great Chinese dynasties after the Han – the Tang at Changan, the Song at Kaifeng, the Ming at Peking.

To appreciate the architecture of the Han palaces we must consult the texts in which they are described and the other arts of that period. There seems, in fact, to have been perfect harmony between sculpture, painting and architecture. That palace halls were decorated with frescoes is attested at a very early date. The Zo Zhuan notes under the year 606 B.C.: 'Duke Ling of Jin levied exorbitant taxes to paint the walls of his palace.' And frescoes have been discovered in tombs of the Han period. Other documents tell us that the Weiyang Palace during the reign of Wu di (140–86 B.C.) had purlins and rafters of scented wood, beams of polished apricot and some doors and pillar bases of jade.

The 'Ming Tang'

The site, which dates from the Western Han Dynasty, was discovered in 1956–7 south of the wall of Changan of the Han (the western suburb of present-day Sian). In its original form it seems to have comprised:
1. a central structure,
2. a wall with four gates and ancillary edifices,
3. a moat outside the wall.

The central structure stood on a rectangular platform that rested in turn on a circular base of rammed earth over 70 yards in diameter. Four halls rose round this vast platform towards the four points of the compass; three had eight annexes but the north hall had only four.

Chinese archaeologists have conjectured that these might be the remains of a ming tang and a bi yong dating from the last years of the Western Han.

A ming tang is a palace designed, in accordance with a theory evolved about the fourth century B.C., as the place chosen for the manifestation of the royal virtue on which the good order of heaven (year, seasons) and earth (government of the people) depended. The structure should have been part of a triple complex:
– the ming tang or sacred hall,
– the bi yong or annular moat,
– the ling tai or transcendental terrace.

The ming tang may have had, in its centre, an empty square space with circular roof but no walls. Each of the four halls arranged around it towards the four cardinal points should be flanked by eight annexes. There, according to the Han philosophers, the ancient kings adjusted their behaviour to that of

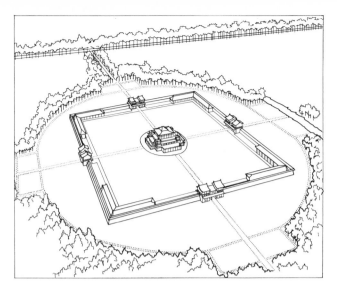

Reconstruction of an architectural ensemble perhaps corresponding to a ming tang and a bi yong, from the traces discovered in 1956–7 south of Changan of the Han

Heaven by moving from one hall to another and changing their costume and diet at each change of season. There they offered sacrifices to the dynastic ancestor and posted the laws at the beginning of each year. In the bi yong, on the other hand, they performed the ceremony of feeding the old men to teach the world filial piety. On the ling tai they scanned the sky to discover lucky or unlucky influences.

The Han emperor Wu built a ming tang at the foot of the Tai shan in 106 B.C. It was a two-storeyed building with a circular upper and a square lower storey. It had no solid wall; its roof was thatched and it was surrounded by a moat full of water, thus combining the two principles of the bi yong and the ming tang. In the year A.D. 4 the usurper Wang Mang built a ming tang at Changan. When the capital was transferred to Luoyang a ming tang was built there and was apparently finished in A.D. 56. The number and location of the halls was closely linked with the symbolic value of numbers. The central edifice was divided into nine halls (recalling the nine provinces); three halls jutted out on each of its four sides ($3 \times 4 =$

12, recalling the 12 positions of the sun). This gave the ensemble the shape of a cross, the four groups of three halls forming the arms and the nine-hall square the centre.

Plan of the Daming Palace in Changan of the Han, from the excavations carried out since 1957

1 Xuanwu men, the main north gate
2 Linde dian
3 Lake Taiyi
4 Hanyuan dian
5 Danfeng Gate

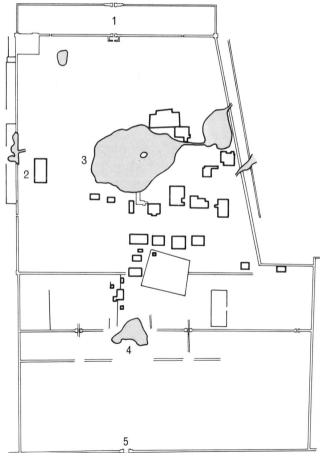

These buildings – ming tang, bi yong and ling tai – were surety for the Royal Virtue and quite separate from the palaces and the temple of the ancestors. Their symbolic significance seems to link them with the imperial temples of later dynasties.

The Palace City of Tang Changan

The imperial palace of the Tang dynasty occupied the centre of the northern section of the city. It faced south and on that side was adjacent to the Imperial City where the government offices were located. As the focal point of the empire, it was the essential part of the capital. In this respect the first words of an edict of A.D. 731 are significant: 'The two capitals are simply the homes of the Emperor.'

The major palace of this Forbidden City was the Taiji gong, which was flanked by smaller palaces to the east and west. The emperor betook himself there on the 1st and 15th of each month to administer the affairs of state. Behind the audience halls other buildings housed the sovereign's private apartments. But, since they stood on low ground, they were very hot in summer. Consequently, in 634 the Tang emperors started to build a new residence, the Daming gong, on higher ground near the north wall. After 662, when it was enlarged, the Daming gong became the emperor's permanent residence.

The method by which the cost of the Daming gong was financed is typical of the procedure followed by Chinese rulers in such cases. The emperor impounded a month's salary of all officials and levied a special tax on the population of fifteen prefectures. Consequently, with the help of conscripted labour the job was finished in a very short time.

Another example of this tyrannical procedure is quoted by the Japanese traveller Ennin, who says that in the 10th month of the year 844 work began on a Terrace of the (Taoist) Immortals 150 feet high; 3,000 legionaries of the left and right armies took part in the work, which was finished on the 3rd day of the 3rd month of 845. 'The top is flat, broad enough to support the foundations of a building with seven bays.... Rocks are arranged on the four sides of the terrace, with grottoes and rocky paths. It is very fine:

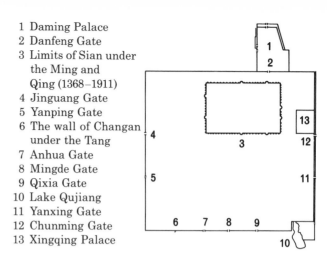

1 Daming Palace
2 Danfeng Gate
3 Limits of Sian under the Ming and Qing (1368–1911)
4 Jinguang Gate
5 Yanping Gate
6 The wall of Changan under the Tang
7 Anhua Gate
8 Mingde Gate
9 Qixia Gate
10 Lake Qujiang
11 Yanxing Gate
12 Chunming Gate
13 Xingqing Palace

Site of the Daming and Xingqing Palaces in Changan of the Tang

planted with pines, thuyas and rare trees. An Imperial edict orders seven Taoist priests to cook the elixir on the terrace and seek immortality.'

The Daming gong covered an area of almost 500 acres. The position of its walls, its chief gates, some twenty buildings and Lake Taiyi was established during several digging campaigns started in 1957. The palace was divided into two parts: the official portion in front, the private apartments behind. The principal edifice of the official portion was the Hanyan dian, the throne room where the major court ceremonies took place and the high officials paid homage to the emperor at New Year and the winter solstice. All that remains today is the platform on which the hall stood. It is 33 feet high, 250 feet wide and 140 feet deep. The hall had eleven bays lengthways and four across. It was surrounded by a covered gallery whose pillars rested in cavities dug in the terrace, and flanked to the east and west by two towers that stood on platforms 50 feet high and were linked with the main hall by covered passageways. Access from the south was by three ramps some 76 yards long.

A short distance to the north-west stood the Linde Hall, one of the largest of the entire palace. Based on a terrace reinforced with brick, it measured 255 feet by 427 and had 164 pillars arranged in 17 rows from north to south and 10 rows from east to west. The hall was divided into three parts, the first two paved with marble slabs, the third with square polished bricks. The emperor often gave banquets there and received his ministers and foreign envoys.

Most of the buildings of the Daming gong, particularly the private apartments situated at the north end, were surrounded by gardens. Documents of the period say that the ensemble had twenty-one gates, twenty-four large halls and over forty towers, pavilions, terraces and kiosks, some designed as government offices, some for study and meditation, some for pleasure.

Another palace, the Xingqing gong, was erected in 714 close to the east wall of the city. Designed for receptions, audiences and banquets, its enclosure comprised a vast oval pool encircled by pavilions and kiosks. Excavations started in 1958 have brought to light traces of halls, galleries and an entrance pavilion in the middle of the south wall.

The recently discovered vestiges of these Tang palaces illustrate the literature of that period and confirm the idea of the sumptuous court of Changan we get from the art of that golden age. It was a period of extraordinary artistic creativity in the fields of calligraphy, painting, music and sculpture. Its works of art, jewelry, ceramics and textiles reflect the unheard-of luxury and the exotic taste that characterized the court. Caravans that started out from Changan carried Chinese products over the routes of Central Asia to the trade centres of the Middle East and returned laden with silks from India, spices from Arabia, horses from Bactria, embroideries and goldsmiths' work from Persia. Ambassadors from all over the world, mountebanks, craftsmen fleeing from the hordes of Islam, gathered in Changan, the intellectual and artistic centre of the Asia of that day.

The Song Palaces

We know very little about the Song palaces. The founder of the dynasty aimed at renewing in Kaifeng the splendours of Changan and summoned Yu Hao,

an architect from the south, to direct building operations there. Yu Hao brought to Henan the curved roof and the structural methods evolved in the southern provinces, which formed the basis of the official Song style. The new buildings were less spacious than those of the Tang – the sovereigns of the eleventh century seem to have had been poorer than their predecessors – and depended more on lightness, refined details, sculptured ornament and colour. There seems to have been a remarkable variety of architectural decoration at that time. The repertory of motifs quoted in Li Jie's treatise on architecture, Ying zao fa shi, comprises geometrical, floral and animal patterns as well as human figures. These last disappeared entirely from pictorial and sculptural decoration under the Ming and Qing, and in this respect too, the Imperial Palace in Peking denotes a decline in comparison with the artistic creations of the Tang and Song.

Painting during the period of the Five Dynasties and the Northern Song may have influenced the style and decoration of contemporary palaces. Documents have preserved the names of painters, like Liu Wentong, who are said to have helped draft the plans for the Kaifeng palaces. Inversely, in Song paintings one finds idealized representations of palaces. The works attributed to Guo Zhongshu, a painter famous for his views of architecture during the Five Dynasties and early Song periods, and those executed in his manner, such as 'The Summer Palace of the Emperor Ming Huang' (Osaka Museum, Japan), are typical of the taste of that time.

The Freer Gallery, Washington, has another painting, probably by a pupil of Li Lung-mien (c. 1040 to 1106). The architecture is light, even airy in its complexity, and very refined in its details. The Museum of Fine Arts, Boston, has a scroll attributed to Zhao Boju entitled 'Entry into Guanzhong of the First Emperor of the Han Dynasty', showing the palaces of Qin Shi huang di as a Song artist imagined them. Zhao Boju, favourite painter of the Emperor Gao Zong (1127–1162), was entrusted with some of the interior decoration. His colourful, archaizing and illustrative manner naturally pleased the Song sovereigns, who preferred warm tones – gold, green, red and blue–for their palaces. This colour scheme, which Zhao Boju borrowed from the Tang painter Li Six un, later influenced Qiu Ying and other Ming artists. We know from documents that the Ming emperors favoured an 'old bronze' green, a deep purple and greenish blue tints that match what we know of Qiu Ying's work. Thus we may form an idea of the iridescent colours of the imperial palaces from the works of Zhao Boju for the Song and Qiu Ying for the Ming.

Peking Palaces of the Yuan Period

The building of the Mongol capital that most impressed Marco Polo and Brother Odoric was the Imperial Palace, which they considered one of the wonders of the world. The Palace, heart of the Imperial City, occupied a rectangular area enclosed by high walls over 2 miles in circumference topped by towers at the corners and gates and flanked by a moat. Its site seems to have been exactly the same as that of the Palace City of the Ming and Qing (now the Museum of the Imperial Palace), which was built on Yuan foundations.

As at Changan and later under the Ming, the big halls of state were erected near the entrance, in what was called the Outer Court. Next came the Inner Court occupied by less important buildings; lastly, at the far end, the Palace City reserved for the residence of the imperial family. The palace area comprised, on the west, Lake Behai and the pleasure grounds that surrounded it.

Though its main lines were in the Song tradition, the Mongol palace displayed some innovations. The use of brick and glazed tiles became general; the system of long galleries joining or surrounding buildings developed; and the erection of points of vantage helped the Mongol aristocracy to control the city.

Peking Palaces of the Ming and Qing

The present-day Imperial Palace (Gugong) was begun in 1406, renovated in the sixteenth century and largely restored from the sixteenth to the nineteenth. But the general layout seems to have undergone very little change. The private apartments occupied till 1924 by the imperial family have been turned into a museum, as has the official part of the palace.

This 'Forbidden City' is a vast rectangle measuring almost 1,100 yards from south to north and 830 from east to west, surrounded by a wall about 23 feet high and a wide moat. The wall is pierced by four gates, each of which has three openings and is topped by a tower. The two main gates, in the middle of the south and north walls, form the two ends of the city's great median spine. The east and west gates are set close enough to the southern corners to give easy access to the offices and audience halls located in the southernmost part of the enclosure. The four corners of the wall are dominated by towers whose roofs are mirrored in the waters of the moat. This latter is separated from the wall by a space that forms a bailey occupied by barracks and depots for the guard.

The palace is sited exactly on the south-north axis and opens towards the south on a long closed courtyard that extends as far as the Tianan men, the gate to the Imperial City, and formerly reached the Qian men. Outside the Tianan men stand two marble columns adorned with coiled dragons and cloud motifs in relief and topped by two wing-like ornaments. The Huabiao, as these columns are called, were apparently symbols of the imperial glory.

The long space that separates the Tianan men from the south gate of the palace, Wu men, is sometimes used for military parades. It is divided into two vast courts separated by the Duan men gate. To the east and west, surrounded by parks, rise the great Temple of the Imperial Ancestors, the Tai miao, and the Shejitan or Altar of the Sun.

The Tai miao, to the east, built by the Emperor Yong le, was restored in 1544 and again in the Qian long reign. The ensemble is encircled by two thick walls, the space between which is planted with pine trees. The central enclosure comprises the main building, the Qian dian, a hall eleven bays wide with a two-deck roof in yellow glazed tiles standing on a three-tier terrace of white marble. Two other, smaller halls stand on a simple marble terrace behind the Qian dian, which is fronted by a vast court lined on both sides by symmetrical buildings.

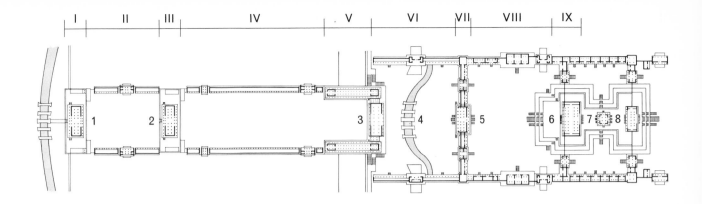

Plan of the official part of the Imperial Palace, Peking, in the Ming and Qing periods

The Official Part of the Palace

The Wu men or South Gate, built in 1420, rebuilt in 1647 and restored in 1801, is the most impressive of all the palace gates. It has a central edifice two storeys high with nine bays on the façade (138 yards long). On each side a long wing juts out towards the south topped by four towers linked by galleries. The two-deck roof of the central building is covered with yellow glazed tiles – the colour reserved for the emperor – and embellished with finials. The gate gives access through three openings to a vast flagged court at the far end of which stands the Taihe men. This outer court is about 655 yards long. The River of Golden Water, Jinshui he, traverses the foreground from east to west in a broad curve crossed by five marble bridges with carved balustrades. The central avenue over the central bridge, which only the em-

peror could use, led straight to the Taihe men (the Gate of Supreme Harmony), whose white marble terrace is reached by three stairways; the central ramp, 60 yards long and embellished with carved dragons, was reserved for the emperor's palanquin. The gatehouse is a hall divided into three naves with nine bays on the open front. Tall pillars support the deep curve of the two-deck roof.

The Hall of Supreme Harmony (Taihe dian) lies about 200 yards beyond the Taihe men. It is the first of the three big ceremonial edifices of the palace, which stand on a vast three-tier terrace. Each tier has a marble balustrade and is punctuated by twin stairways separated by a ramp.

The Taihe dian, built in 1627, rebuilt in 1697 and repaired in 1765, is the most stately edifice of this part of the palace. It is 211 feet (11 bays) long, 121 feet (5 bays) deep and 88 feet high. The interior is divided along the major axis by four rows of eight pillars each and the southernmost bay forms an open verandah. The two-deck hipped roof is covered with yellow tiles. This hall was used for important ceremonies like the emperor's enthronement, court homage to the sovereign (on New Year's Day, the winter solstice, the emperor's birthday, and when generals left for war), and the promulgation of important decrees.

The Zhonghe dian (the Hall of Middle Harmony), rebuilt in 1627 and restored in 1765, stands half-way between the Taihe dian and the Baohe dian. It is a square pavilion measuring about 52 feet across. Four big inner pillars support the pyramidal roof and divide the hall into three naves. The emperor passed through the Zhonghe dian before attending important ceremonies in the Taihe dian. It was there that the messages read at commemorative functions in the ancestral temple were drafted. There, too, farm implements and new seed were presented to the emperor once a year.

The Baohe dian (the Hall of Protecting Harmony) dates from the same period and is built in the same style. But it is bigger (160 × 75 feet) and has the same plan as the Taihe dian. The double roof is half-hipped. Here the emperor in person examined the candidates to the Hanlin Academy, granted audiences and received the vassal princes.

The Outer Court, in which these three formal buildings lie, is enclosed by a wall with galleries; those on the south contained the imperial libraries and storerooms.

The Private Part of the Palace

The main entrance to the Inner Court, Da Nei, is the Qianqing Gate, a one-storey pavilion with five bays on the façade standing on a marble terrace. The principal edifices of this private part of the palace were rebuilt in 1655. The axial avenue continues northwards dotted by three great halls that balance the three official halls of the Outer Court. The first is the Palace of Celestial Purity, Qianqing gong, which was the emperor's personal residence during the Ming period. After the Kang xi reign of the Qing dynasty it was there that he received officials and the envoys of subject states. The hall has a two-deck hipped roof, nine bays on the façade and is divided into three naves. It was burnt down in 1514 and again in 1596, rebuilt in 1655, repaired in 1669, destroyed by fire again in 1797 and rebuilt to the original plan.

The Palace of Earthly Peace, Kunning gong, the empress's residence under the Ming, was designed along the same lines. Under the Qing it no longer served as the nuptial chamber of the emperor and empress.

Between these two halls there was a square pavilion, the Jiaotai dian, that resembled the Zhonghe dian of the Outer Court. It was originally the empress's

throne room and from the Qian long reign onwards the seals of the dead emperors were kept there.

A magnificent garden, the Yuhua Yuan, extended behind the Kunning gong. At each side of this central area a number of pavilions built round courtyards served as apartments for the emperor, empresses, concubines and eunuchs. From the Kang xi reign on the emperor's apartments were located in the Yangxin dian, the Hall of Spiritual Nutriment, on the west side of the Inner Court. Two pavilions to the north of this edifice served respectively for the empress and the imperial concubine. Still farther north were the residences of the imperial princesses, while the north-west corner of the Palace City was arranged as a vast park, the 'xi yuan'.

Heating and Water Supply

The emperor used water from the west suburbs. The other inhabitants of the palace were served by seventy or eighty wells. Inside the palace the rainwater was drained off through a complicated system of canals. Each pavilion had its own branch, which was connected with the main conduits. These latter flowed into the River of Golden Water and the culverts under the north wall of the Forbidden City, which flowed in turn into the moat outside the wall.

Under the Ming, heating conduits were installed under the floor in most of the palace halls. They branched out from a furnace located under the flagged pavement of the courtyard or in the basement of the hall itself. The hot air produced by the furnace circulated through pipes and heated the hall uniformly without fumes or smoke.

The Spatial Layout

Present-day travellers – and in this they are luckier than the inhabitants of Peking under the empire – can view the Palace from the top of Coal Hill, Mei shan, which was formerly part of the Palace territory though it lay outside the ramparts.

To build their Palace City the Ming emperors imported timber from Yunnan, Sichuan and Guizhou (for pillars and beams), stone from Hebei (Zhuozhou and Fang shan), marble from Xuzhou, bricks from Linqing and Suzhou (Jiangsu). The white terraces, the red buildings and the yellow roofs harmonize with the green foliage of the courtyards. The walls, coated with a red wash weathered by rain and frost, range through all the shades from vermilion to pink and rusty brown.

I do not wish to revert to the symmetrical arrangement along the south-north axis and its two sides, which here is so clear to see. But I must comment on the gradual unfolding of this extraordinary composition. From the Qian men to the Taihe dian a series of five gates (Daqing men, Tianan men, Duan men, Wu men and Taihe men) give access to six enclosures of various shapes and sizes dominated by three buildings of the first importance – Tianan men, Wu men and Taihe dian. These are the three climaxes of the palace architecture. Each is preceded by an introduction in the shape of a low transitional edifice ushered in by a small courtyard. Thus, between the Tianan men and the Wu men there is a rather small square courtyard, then the Duan men, followed by a vast rectangular courtyard extending northwards to the Wu men, which constitutes the second climax. The same sequence is repeated between the Wu men and the Taihe dian: a rectangular court, then the Taihe men, followed by a vast space that accentuates the importance of the Taihe dian, which forms the third climax. In this alternating rhythm, based on an initial climax, a pause and a second climax, the role of this last in the aesthetic, functional and ceremonial planes is given maximum emphasis.

The Imperial Temples of Peking

These sacrificial altars, where the emperor offered prayers in honour of the powers of nature, were usually situated outside the city. Thus in the fifteenth century, when work started on the edifices of the Temple of Heaven, the site was a suburb.

The situation of these temples was determined by a symbolism that linked orientation, colour and the season of the year.
– East (to the left looking southwards) = spring = green;
– West = autumn = white;
– South = summer = red;
– North = winter = black.

Under the Ming and Qing two of the most impressive imperial temples stood to right and left of the triumphal way in the southern suburb of Peking – the Temple of Heaven on the left (looking south) and the Temple of Agriculture on the right. The Temple of Earth was located to the north of the city, the Temple of the Sun to the east and the Temple of the Moon to the west.

Certain colours were used predominantly in the decoration of certain temples – blue in the Temple of Heaven, red in the Temple of the Sun, white in the Temple of the Moon.

These temples comprised four major elements:
1. an altar (tan), in the shape of a circular or rectangular terrace of one or more storeys fenced with marble balustrades, which occupied the centre of an enclosure and was encircled by a wall;
2. an imperial temple, where the tablets were kept except when sacrifices were offered;
3. various buildings used as storerooms for ritual paraphernalia, kitchens for preparing viands, etc.

The Temple of Heaven, Tian tan

This is the only imperial temple of Peking that is well preserved. It was built in 1420 and restored in 1530 and 1751. The whole enclosure, surrounded by a double wall, measures about 1,860 yards by 1,750. The outer wall, about 4 miles in circumference, bounds a first enclosure, a timbered park interspersed with fields where the animals bred for the sacrifices were pastured. The wall, whose corners are rounded on the north, has two triple portals on the west side through which the temple is reached from the south-north axis of the city. A second, inner wall 2½ miles long bounds a second enclosure that contains the buildings of the temple proper and is divided into two parts which served different purposes. The south part, with the altar in the centre, was the place where the emperor celebrated the sacrifice to Heaven. In the north part, round the Qinian dian, the emperor prayed Heaven each spring for a good harvest.

These two precincts are linked by an avenue 100 feet wide and paved with bricks which forms the median axis. The surrounding trees give the composition a third dimension.

The Altar of Heaven

This vast circular altar derives from the mound (tai), which from the earliest times was the classic site of the cult of Heaven, Earth and the Sun God. It is formed by three stepped terraces paved with white marble and each fenced by a white marble balustrade. The total height is almost 16 feet. At each of the four cardinal points a stairway gives access to the three terraces. The altar is girded by a low (6 feet) circular wall topped with glazed tiles. At the foot of each stairway a three-arched portico opens on to a sacred grove. A second low wall, similar to the first and broken by porticoes coaxial with those already mentioned, limits a second enclosure, which is not round but square.

The Huang Qiongyu

This building, located in another round enclosure to the north of the altar, formerly contained the tablets of Heaven and of the dead emperors. The circular building stands in the centre of a courtyard on a plain white marble terrace. It rests on a double circle of eight pillars. Those of the outer row are joined together by curved beams, those of the inner row by straight beams that support the vast conical roof, which is covered with dark-blue glazed tiles. Two buildings of five bays each, to the east and west, served for storing the paraphernalia used in the sacrifices.

The Qinian dian
(The Hall for Prayers for an Abundant Harvest)

This temple, which is also built to a circular plan (85 feet across at the base), has a triple roof. Originally, under the Ming, the three roofs were of different colours: the top one blue, the middle one yellow, the bottom one green. In 1751, during the Qian long reign, they were made over entirely in blue tiles. The under sides of the eaves are bluish green.

Three rows of pillars form the essential element of the structure. Those of the outer row support the lowest section of the roof and serve as flying buttresses for the twelve pillars of the second row, which are far less tall and are linked four by four by robust tie-beams. In the centre stand four very tall (63 feet) pillars that are linked with those of the second row at the meeting point of the tie-beams and to each other by semicircular beams. The conception of this framework is very daring on so vast a scale.

The Qinian dian stands on a three-stepped terrace of white marble reached by eight stairways. On each side of the temple are two buildings of nine bays each covered with dark-blue tiles.

The Qinian dian is followed, along the south-north axis, by the Huangqian dian, annexes and furnaces.

The Zhai gong

This Palace for Purification is located in the northwest part of the second enclosure; it was used by the emperor before offering a sacrifice and comprises a throne room flanked by other buildings to the right and left. The whole is surrounded by a moat and a double wall that isolate the palace entirely from the outside world.

Sacrifices to Heaven were offered in the first month of spring to obtain a bumper harvest, in the first month of summer to ask for the normal rainfall needed by the crops, and on special occasions (in periods of drought or to give thanks to Heaven). The offerings were of different kinds – animals, cooked viands or symbolic objects.

This handsome ensemble, whose curving blue roofs harmonize with the nearby cedars and cypresses, is undoubtedly one of the most perfect embodiments of the Chinese monumental conception. Here, more than in the Imperial Palace, successive restorations have respected the grandeur of the composition and the sober elegance of the original structure.

Plates

Pagodas and Monasteries

Detail of a mural painting in cave 140 (right-hand wall) at Dunhuang (Gansu), representing pilgrims outside a pagoda.

Entrance to Tangzi cave at Longmen (Henan). Northern Wei (early sixth century); it was restored under the early Tang (seventh century).

Models of pavilions and pagodas carved in the rock at Longmen (Henan).

Sian: the Dayan ta or Great Wild Goose Pagoda (652–704). It stood in the south-east section of the Tang capital Changan.

Sian: the Dayan ta. One is impressed by the vigorous volumes and sober ornamentation.

The Heli ta (937–75) of the Qixia monastery north-east of Nanking.

The Qixia Monastery (Qixia si) was founded in 487 on a magnificent site at the foot of a wooded hill. Except for the Heli ta, all the buildings now standing date from late nineteenth century.

The twin pagodas (Shuang ta) erected at Suzhou between 984 and 987. The octagonal seven-storey pagodas are built of brick in imitation of timber.

The Huqiu Pagoda (961) also called the Yunyan Temple Pagoda, north-west of Suzhou.

The pagoda of the Tianning si (Temple of Heavenly Peace) in Peking dates from the early twelfth century. During the Liao period it stood inside the wall of the capital. The temple of which it formed a part has disappeared.

Pavilion for playing chess on one of the peaks of the Hua shan (Shânxi).

8–9 Liuhe ta, the Pagoda of the Six Harmonies, on the bank of the Qiantang jiang at Hangzhou (Zhejiang). It is almost 200 feet high with seven storeys outside and thirteen inside. The sober lines of its dark-red woodwork match the elegance of its curving roofs.

120 Suzhou (Jiangsu): the Beisi ta, Pagoda of the Temple of Gratitude (Baoen si), built in the middle of the twelfth century to replace one destroyed by the Jin in 1130.

121 The Wuta si, Temple of the Five Pagodas, in the north-west suburb of Peking. All that remains of the temple is the hall of the five pagodas built in 1473. The decoration of the arched portal recalls that of the Juyong guan (Pl. 28).

Tombs

122 A small funerary ensemble east of Luoyang (Henan) not yet identified.

123 The tomb of the first Ming emperor (Hong wu) at Nanking (late fourteenth century). Stairway leading to the terrace, which backs up against the mound.

124 Statue of a civil official on the Way of the Spirits in the Ming tombs (Shisan ling), Peking.

125 Part of the Animal Way in the Ming tombs, Peking. Fabulous beast (xiechi), camels and elephants.

126 White marble arch (shipai fang) erected in 1540 as entrance to the Way of the Spirits in the Ming tombs.

127 Stele before the Dingling, the tomb of the Emperor Wan li (1563–1620). The tortoise is a symbol of immortality.

128 Shisan ling, Peking. The Lingen dian (Pavilion of Eminent Favours) of the Changling, the tomb of the Emperor Yong le (1403–24).

129 Ming Tombs, Peking: the Tower of the Soul (ming-lou) supported by the square tower (fangcheng) of the Changling. This tower contains the stele with the name of the emperor buried under the mound (here Yong le).

130 Burial chamber of the Dingling, the tomb of the Emperor Wan li, opened in 1956. The coffins of the emperor and his two empresses lay on a stone dais.

Plans

Notes

A Brief Summary of Chinese Spatial Symbolism

Architecture, like all other symbol systems, is typical of a certain order of civilization. The Chinese civilization is one of hierarchized, regulated relationships in a universe that is not organized in the service of man but after whose likeness man, with a view to integrating himself better in it, has created a complete system of correspondences. Fields, cities and houses must be oriented like the square earth, each side of which corresponds to a cardinal point.

If insistence on orientation of palaces and cities implies an organization of society modelled on that of the universe, the orientation of tombs denotes that burial and space are interdependent. This is emphasized under the Han by the presence of the symbols of the four regions (the green dragon of the east, the red bird of the south, the white tiger of the west and the black tortoise of the north) on the columns that limit burial grounds.

This symbolism relates man's final resting place to the universe, 'a universe in perpetual palpitation through the creative interplay of Yin and Yang'. The concept of Yin and Yang reflects the concrete, antithetic aspects of space and time. Yin stands for the shady slopes of mountains, for cold rainy weather, for the right hand, for all that is feminine and passive; Yang for the sunny side, for heat and drought, for the left hand, for all that is masculine and active. Universal harmony is the sum of these opposite and complementary energies. Man is conditioned by this rhythm of a nature that is in a constant state of flux. In China the human space was made to harmonize as far as possible with the rhythm of nature. This spatial integration did not deny man the role of organizer, for he acted on time and space through a quantity of interconnected symbols. In ancient times, since gates and cardinal points coincided, it sufficed for the sovereign to welcome each season at a different gate of his capital in order to control the universal machine. The chain of symbols seemed infinitely comprehensive and coherent.

The four cardinal points and the centre correspond to the five elements, the five heavens, the five species of animals, musical notes, odours, numbers, places of sacrifices, bodily organs, colours, flavours. This makes it obvious that these correspondences confer common properties on whole series of phenomena and situations and offer the possibility of acting on one or the other. For instance:

cardinal point = north
element = water
colour = black
flavour = salty
odour = musty
vegetable food = yellow millet
domestic animal = pig
part of house = path (or well)
number = six
organ = kidneys
virtue = wisdom
emblem = moon
season = winter

Man's insertion in the space-time continuum is perfect and his security is absolute because everything is determined and explained. All man has to do is to integrate himself in his proper place in the hierarchical order, which is at once stable and in perpetual evolution.

The idea that space and time share a common rhythmic constitution and the belief in the universal efficacy of rhythm, which is the basis of the concept of Yin and Yang, explain the importance of simple oppositions and alternations, of symmetry in respect of a median axis. They also explain the value attributed to the centre (the palace in the centre of the capital, the courtyard as the centre of the dwelling). Lastly, the idea of rhythm is associated with that of cycle, transit, circuit, crystallized both in the triumphal way of a capital and in the twisting path that leads to the aesthetic discovery of a garden.

114

122

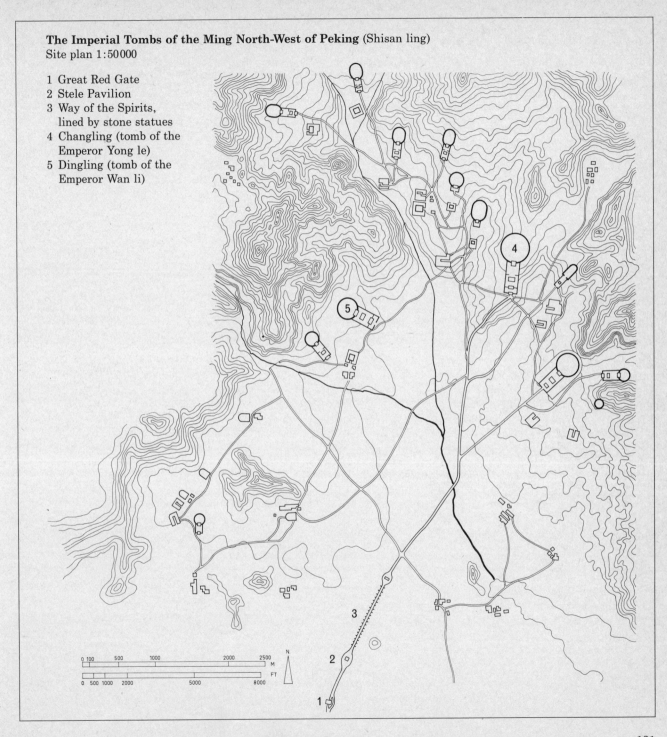

The Imperial Tombs of the Ming North-West of Peking (Shisan ling)
Site plan 1:50000

1 Great Red Gate
2 Stele Pavilion
3 Way of the Spirits,
  lined by stone statues
4 Changling (tomb of the
  Emperor Yong le)
5 Dingling (tomb of the
  Emperor Wan li)

4

5

0 100   500   1000   2000   2500
                                      M

0 500 1000 2000   5000   8000
                                    FT

N.

3

2

1

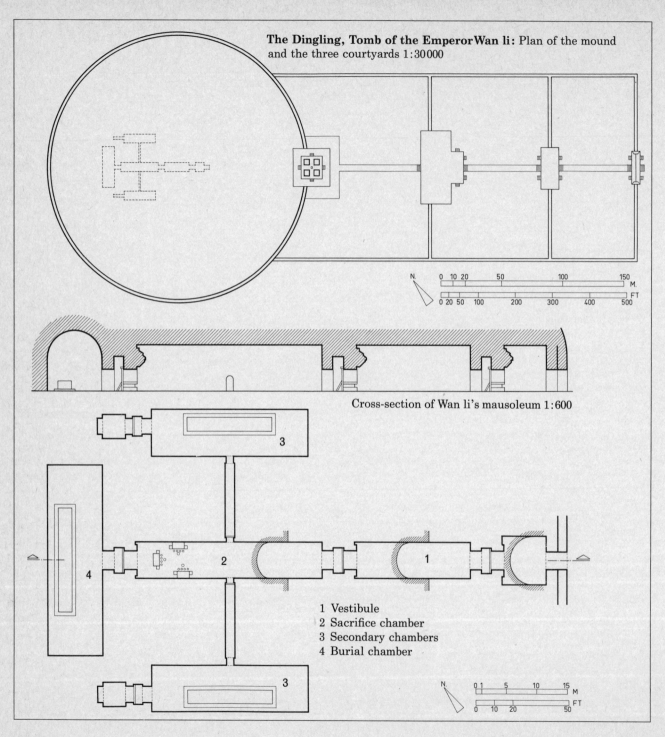

The Dingling, Tomb of the Emperor Wan li: Plan of the mound and the three courtyards 1:30000

Cross-section of Wan li's mausoleum 1:600

1 Vestibule
2 Sacrifice chamber
3 Secondary chambers
4 Burial chamber

4. Religious and Funerary Architecture

Religious Architecture

In China religious architecture comprises Buddhist temples and pagodas as well as Confucian and Taoist temples. From the purely architectural viewpoint there is no great difference between Taoist, Confucian and Buddhist temples. The plan whose main lines we have seen in the Foreword (symmetry relative to a median axis, arrangement of the buildings round a courtyard) was adopted by all three. I shall dwell chiefly on the architectural evolution of the Buddhist temples and pagodas, which have been studied more thoroughly than the Confucian or Taoist. Most Buddhist sanctuaries were completed by buildings for the use of the monks. Hence the plan of a monastery comprises the temple (on the central axis) and its monastic annexes.

The Typical Plan of a Buddhist Monastery (si)

This plan has merely general validity because it takes no account of the variations due to social and cultural factors, which were linked with the particular sect involved, the role of the superior, who could modify or transform the plan, the impact of local architecture, the requirements of the fengshui, and the strife between Buddhists, Taoists and Confucians. During the first half of the fifteenth century, for instance, the Taoists occupied 482 Buddhist monasteries, which they adapted for their own use and only returned to their rightful owners later.

In the commonest plan the buildings are arranged in three groups forming three longitudinal axes. Those on the median axis were the official part of the monastery, open to the public. The two lateral groups housed the monks and the administrative offices.

The entrance to a monastery is usually to the south and the main gate is protected against evil spirits by a screen wall (yingbi). In some cases it is flanked by two towers, one containing a bell, the other a drum. The first building on the median axis is the entrance hall (shan men), which houses the statues of the two guardians of the gate. Next comes the hall of the four heavenly kings (tianwang dian) who guarded the four cardinal points. This edifice is followed by the main hall, its central altar occupied by a statue of the Sakyamuni Buddha or a triad. The images of eighteen (or sixteen) Lohan (ascetics) or the twenty-four Deva (tutelary gods) were often lined up along the walls. The central altar is often placed against a screen that extends to right and left. Behind the screen a second altar facing in the opposite direction is consecrated to a god who may vary from one sect to another but is usually Guanyin (the goddess of mercy, an avatar of Avalokitesvara, the compassionate Bodhisattva).

After the main hall, along the same median axis, comes, as a rule, a two-storey building whose upper floor houses the library and whose ground floor contains the Hall of Meditation (chantang) or of the Law (fatang).

In monasteries where monks were frequently ordained a special building was set aside for that purpose. The position of this hall, which was completed by an ordination terrace, varies from one monastery to another but, whether it is located on the median axis or on one of the other two, it always stands by itself.

The buildings on the median axis serve various purposes. They may be halls for receiving guests or holding the tablets of former superiors, and refectories or dormitories for guests or the monastery employees.

The two lateral axes were reserved for the private use of the community – offices, granaries, kitchens, baths, quarters for the sick, dormitories for the monks, schoolrooms. There is often a Hall of the Five Hundred Lohan, ascetics whose cult became popular at the end of the Tang and the beginning of the Song periods.

The Site of the Pagoda

In the days of the Six Dynasties the pagoda was apparently the centre of religious worship. It stood alone on the median axis before the Hall of the Buddha. This arrangement may perhaps derive, as Professor Soper suggests, from a custom adopted in the great oases of Xinjiang. A Chinese pilgrim named Fa Xian, who visited Khotan in A.D. 400, observed this arrangement (a tower preceding a hall) in an ensemble outside the town.

Under the Sui and the Tang there were two pagodas in the major Buddhist establishments, east and west of the median axis. This formula, dictated by the Chinese passion for symmetry, was abandoned when the Tang economy declined. From then on, with a few exceptions in Southern China, the pagoda – where there was one – was placed behind the main hall or on one of the lateral axes of the monastic ensemble.

Buddhist Architecture from the Fifth to the Tenth Century

Though introduced during the first century A.D., Buddhism long remained the religion of small foreign communities settled in China. It was probably in the north, at the end of the Central Asian routes by which the new religion had arrived, that Buddhist devotion and worship first produced works of art in the fourth century, namely the sculptures and paintings in the rock-cut temples at Dunhuang after 353.

Buddhist rock-cut temples multiplied during the fifth century: at Yungang work started in 450, at Longmen in 495. At the same time temples and monasteries spread in the towns and countryside. A first climax in building operations occurred during the first thirty years of the sixth century. At Luoyang Buddhist establishments grew from a hundred or so in 476 to 1,367 about 534. At that time the dynasties in the north and south competed not only on the political plane but also in the matter of good works and artistic patronage. There was another boom period from the second half of the seventh century to the beginning of the eighth, but the total number of monasteries large and small remained virtually unchanged from the middle of the sixth century (30,000 to 40,000) to the end of the thirteenth (some 42,000). Except for the very big monasteries (some 4,000 from the end of the sixth to the middle of the ninth century), most communities counted between twenty and fifty monks or even fewer.

The richest monasteries and the largest architectural ensembles were erected at the expense of the state, but from the fifth century on a great many were built by nobles and high officials. This led to the proclamation, early in the sixth century, of decrees curbing private building. The reason was that the quantity of metal consumed (for statues, bells and ornaments) withdrew capital from more productive uses and peasant labour from agriculture. The situation became alarming at the end of the seventh century and the beginning of the eighth, when the love of ostentation, a passion for expenditure and the mania for building were reflected in religious and secular edifices alike. Buddhist devotion led individuals and groups to build monasteries and temples, which became places of pilgrimage, centres of merrymaking on festive occasions as well as sanctuaries of peace and quiet.

Temples and Monasteries from the Fifth to the Tenth Century

Little is known about the evolution of architecture under the Six Dynasties and the Tang. Since most timber structures have disappeared, all we know about them derives from the paintings in the Dunhuang cave temples, contemporary Japanese representations, the carved lintel of the Dayan ta and the vestiges of the Foguang si on the Wutai shan.

A fresco in cave no. 130 at Dunhuang, whose style dates it to the second half of the sixth century, represents a temple encircled by a high wall, its gate topped by a pavilion that must have served as a watchtower. The enclosure comprises two courtyards, each with a building in the centre. The symmetrical arrangement is not based on the median axis typical of later temples. Other frescoes at Dunhuang seem to confirm that at the beginning of the Tang period neither median axis nor symmetrical layout had the importance they attained after the middle years of the dynasty.

The Foguang si (Wutai shan, Shanxi)

In June 1937 Professor Liang Sseu-ch'eng discovered on one of the big horizontal beams of the main hall of the Foguang si a long inscription with the name of the founder – a woman. He found the same name with the date 857 on a stone column before the hall. These discoveries proved that this was the oldest large timber structure of the Tang period still in existence.

Wutai shan, the Mountain of the Five Terraces, was one of the chief centres of Buddhism in China and one of the most famous places of pilgrimage. The Buddha Manjusri was worshipped there. During the Six Dynasties and Tang periods many rich monasteries were situated on the mountain. The richest and most popular were rebuilt periodically and, as they stand today, date from the Ming and Qing. Some of the more modest establishments, which had fewer visitors, have preserved their original aspect.

One of these is the Foguang si (the Monastery of the Light of the Buddha), which is located at the head of a wild glen. Facing west, like the glen, the monastery is built on two levels. The lower part originally comprised two halls arranged symmetrically to right and left – the Wenshu dian (restored under the Jin in 1137) and the Quanyin dian. The main hall (Zheng dian), which has seven bays on the façade and two in depth, occupies the upper level and dominates the whole monastery. Behind it, on the right, several octagonal, circular and hexagonal pagodas rise on the mountain-side.

Founded under the Wei dynasty between 471 and 499, the monastery was burnt down during the persecutions of 845 and rebuilt a few years later, probably between 850 and 860. It is almost a miracle that the main hall is still extant. Its single storey is girdled by thick brick walls for protection against the winter cold and its façade is pierced by five doors and two groups of lattice windows. The hipped roof rests directly on the purlins and has a very gentle slope that gets steeper towards the summit. The eaves are supported by a system of brackets whose columnar clusters are so massive that they occupy about one-third of the height from the floor to the rafters. The intermediate clusters are simpler and this gives the façade an alternating rhythm of strong and weak accents. The interior is divided into a nave and two aisles that are lower than the nave.

The Japanese building that most closely resembles the main hall of the Foguang si is the Kondō or main hall of the Tōshōdaiji Temple near Nara, built in the last third of the eighth century or the first years of the ninth. The two buildings have similar dimensions and volume; both measure seven bays by four; both have a hipped roof, though the Japanese is slightly higher than the Chinese; and what I have just said about the hall of the Foguang si also applies to the Kondō of the Tōshōdaiji. The differences between the two are probably due to their different dating. The columnar bracket clusters of the Kondō epitomize Tang architectural teaching in Japan. The Foguang si, instead, forestalls the Song style by doubling the cluster in height with two parallel slanting arms (ang). Moreover, the corner clusters have three slanting arms on the diagonal axis. Lastly, the intermediate clusters, instead of being formed by a simple two-tier strut as in the Japanese temple, differ from the columnar clusters only by a greater simplicity which prefigures the single system repeated along the entire façade under the Song. On the lintel of the Dayan ta (Sian, Shânxi) the columnar brackets still alternate with intermediate struts.

The origins of the Chinese pagoda, from Willetts, 'Chinese Art'

a Pottery model of a watchtower, Han dynasty
b The Great Stūpa at Sāñchī, India (c. 50 B.C.)
c Reliquary stūpa at Gandhāra (c. A.D. 200)
d 'Indian' pagoda from a fresco at Dunhuang (fifth to sixth centuries)

Pagodas (ta)

In China pagodas were erected for votive or commemorative purposes, or to hold relics. They derive from two sources – one properly speaking Chinese, the other Indian.

The multi-storeyed pavilions surrounded by balconies of the Han period prefigure the ting type pagoda, which consists of a number of superposed square timber pavilions that decrease slightly in size from the ground up. Multi-storeyed structures of this type are represented on bas-reliefs at Yungang and Longmen. The five-storey timber pagoda of the Hōryūji Temple at Nara (Japan), built at the beginning of the seventh century, also belongs to the same type.

In India we find that the most sacred edifice of a monastery is the stūpa, designed to hold the relics of the Buddha. At Sāñchī (second century B.C. to first century A.D.) the oldest Indian stūpas have a brick dome (anda) topped by a square stone coffer (harmikā), above which rises a mast with three ceremonial umbrellas (chattra) that symbolize the spiritual royalty of the person whose relics are buried under the stūpa. During the first centuries of our era the custom of erecting stūpas spread through north-west India. As their proportions grew they came to resemble the śikhara towers. Most of them are now mere heaps of rubble, but we know what they looked like from small votive bronzes that were exported at least

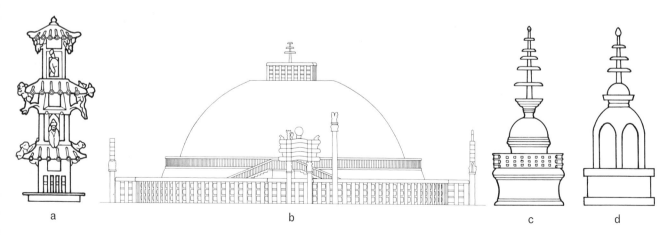

a   b   c   d

as early as the sixth century. An Indian-type stūpa is featured in one of the Dunhuang frescoes raised aloft on a single-storeyed Chinese pavilion of the ting type. Gradually the Chinese eliminated all but the mast, leaving at its foot the merest trace of the stūpa. The pagoda was made up of two elements – the infrastructure in timber and masonry and the superstructure formed by the stūpa.

The Indian śikhara, a conical roof designed to shelter the statue of a god, also influenced the development of the Chinese pagodas. These latter, initially made of wood, from the sixth century on were more and more frequently of brick or stone, which may also have been due to an Indian influence. The oldest brick pagoda still extant in China is that of the Songyue si, built in 523 on a terrace of the Song shan (Henan), which was an important place of worship under the Northern Wei. Presumably based on an Indian model, it has an octagonal plan and two main storeys separated by a cornice of corbelled bricks. The corners of the second storey are embellished with hexagonal brick pillars. Each side has a false façade with arched windows, above which are two crouching lions in low niches. The conical top is divided by cornices into fifteen sham storeys. The jutting cornices are typical of the brick structures of the period. The supple design, so admirably suited to the material, testifies to the progress made in masonry construction under the impulse of Buddhism. The interior of the building, which is 131 feet tall, is divided into ten storeys separated by timber floors.

If the Songyue si pagoda has the aspect of a Chinese version of the Indian śikhara, the four-door Simen ta pagoda of the Shentong si at Licheng (Shandong) is an example of the ting type. It dates from 544 and is the oldest existing stone pagoda in China. The roof of the square shrine, which resembles a timber ting in stone, has several tiers of corbels topped by a stūpa. Each side has a doorway crowned by a semi-circular arch. The weight of the stūpa is supported by a square central pier on each side of which a Buddha is carved.

The only Tang buildings still extant on the site of the ancient Changan are brick pagodas dating from the middle years of the dynasty. The largest and finest

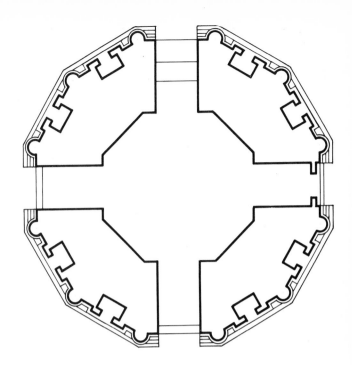

Plan of the Songyue temple pagoda at Song shan (Henan) built in 523

is the Dayan ta (the Great Wild Goose Pagoda) of the Temple of Great Benevolence (Dacien si) north-west of Lake Qujiang. On his return from India in 649 the pilgrim Xuanzang took up his abode in the monastery in order to translate the Buddhist canons. At his suggestion a five-storey pagoda was erected there in 652 for keeping the precious texts he had brought back from his travels. It was given the name of Jing ta (Pagoda of the Classics). Xuanzang's biography states that the building was based on an Indian model, perhaps the Bodh-Gayā, which he had visited. The pagoda was partially rebuilt with ten storeys between 701 and 704 but only seven were left when it was restored in 930–33.

It is a sturdy square brick tower 197 feet high and 84 feet across at the base, standing on a terrace 18 feet high. The extremely thick mud walls are faced with yellow bricks carefully laid, though the courses are irregular. Inside, a wooden stairway leads to the upper floors. Outside, the severely plain facing is relieved by slender pilasters, ten on each side of the ground floor, eight on the first, six on the second and third, four on the last three. On each side there is a doorway with a semicircular arch on the ground floor, matched by a window of similar design on each of the upper floors. On the black marble lintel over each door is engraved a scene from the life of the Buddha. The one on the west side, which is particularly fine and well preserved, represents Sakyamuni Buddha seated in the attitude of preaching surrounded by Bodhisattvas in a single-storey pavilion – an invaluable example of timber architecture of the Tang period. The cornices of the seven storeys of the pagoda are formed by courses of corbelled bricks set like an inverted stairway and edged with a zig-zag pattern of bricks laid cornerwise.

Not far from the Dayan ta there is another brick pagoda, the Xiaoyan ta (the Small Wild Goose Pagoda), erected in 707 for one of the best known monasteries in Changan. This square pagoda also reflects the Tang taste for clear, simple language. It stands on a tall base and today has thirteen storeys (150 feet high) of the original fifteen. On the ground-floor two arched doorways open on the north and south sides; they are matched by windows on the upper floors. The walls are thinner than in the Dayan ta, but are also made of mud faced with yellow bricks. The horizontal separations of the storeys are like those of the Dayan ta.

The Jingchuang

Early in the Tang period it became the custom to raise on the right and left of a Buddhist hall or temple a pair of octagonal pillars engraved with dhārani (magic formulas), called jingchuang. They ranged in height from 10 to 20 feet and consisted of a base adorned with niches and lotus petals, a shaft engraved with the dhārani, and an ornamental apex. An example exists in the courtyard of the Foguang si on Mount Wutai erected in 877.

These small octagonal structures may have influenced the shape of the pagodas, which, after being mostly square under the Tang, became octagonal in the tenth century. Two other jingchuang built in 969 stand before the Tianwang Hall (or Daxiongbao dian) of the Lingyin si at Hangzhou (Zhejiang). They are decorated with Buddhist reliefs and their nine storeys are marked by roofs that imitate timber structures, with the eaves supported by bracket clusters. The traditional use of timber as building material influenced stone and brick constructions increasingly under the Five Dynasties and the Song. This is clear to see in the Heli ta of the Qixia si at Nanking, built between 937 and 975. It is a small stona pagoda (about 50 feet high) whose plinth is decorated with bas-reliefs representing the eight moments of the Buddha's life in compositions and building forms typical of the Five Dynasties period. The shaft of the pagoda stands on a lotus-petal base, and on its eight sides are carved the four guardian kings, deities and sham doors. Five stone roofs, one above the other, imitating those of a timber building, crown the shaft and are separated by rows of niches containing images of the Buddha. Stylistically, this handsome pagoda is very close to the jingchuang of the Lingyin si in architecture and decoration alike. Both display elements typical of tenth-century architecture in Southern China.

The Religious Architecture of the Song Period

In the tenth century there was a Buddhist renaissance that continued in the north-east under the barbarian dynasties of the Liao and Jin and in the rest of the country under the Song. New monasteries were built, and ancient institutions were restored or enlarged, as on the Wutai shan (Shanxi) and the Omei shan (Sichuan).

Pagodas

Some sixty pagodas dating from the Five Dynasties and the Song are still extant. Most of them are octagonal and their design is derived from timber structures.

The twin pagodas of the Shuang ta at Suzhou (Jiangsu) resulted from the doubling of the pagoda to the east and west of the temple's median axis. The stūpa, complete with dome and umbrellas, still crowns the octagonal edifice.

The Huqiu pagoda, also at Suzhou, was finished in 961. It is an octagonal structure in brick 154 feet high, whose seven storeys are adorned with brackets. Each side has a cinquefoil window and the corners are marked by small engaged pillars. Inside the base an octagonal deambulatory surrounds a square central hall whose walls and brackets are enhanced with ochre and pale blue paint.

The Iron Pagoda (Tie ta) of the Youguo monastery at Kaifeng (Henan) is of the same type. The monastery has disappeared but the pagoda, which owes its name to the colour of its glazed brick, still stands in the north-east section of the city. It was built in 1049, is 177 feet high and has thirteen storeys. Each corner is marked by a pillar, and the sham windows of each storey are adorned with a recess containing a Buddha. The same decoration is repeated on the octagonal pagoda of the Kaiyan si at Dingxian (Hebei). But the Iron Pagoda is remarkable for the scroll patterns and Bodhisattvas stamped on the bricks before glazing. The monument is a unique example of the taste for ornamentation that predominated in the architecture of the Northern Song.

At the opposite stylistic pole is the pagoda of the Baima si, near Luoyang (Henan), built in 1175. Its square groundplan, its thirteen storeys marked by simple brick corbelling, its lack of decoration and its severe design are still inspired by Tang models.

The preponderance of timber buildings at that time led to the erection of pagodas in which brick and wood were employed side by side. Two examples of this are the Ruiguang ta and the Beisi ta at Suzhou, which date from the middle of the twelfth century. The main structure is of brick, whereas the brackets, roof and balustrades are of wood. This gives them an appearance of lightness and a certain resemblance to those built entirely of wood. These latter include the Shijia ta of the Fogong si at Yingxian (Shanxi), a very big octagonal pagoda 220 feet tall, built in 1056. Its nine timber storeys stand on a brick base that has a square lower part and an octagonal upper part. The four middle storeys have a balcony and a lean-to roof; the top storey has a very rich bracket system that testifies to the quality of the bracketing at that time. The stūpa that crowns the building is of the Liao type: two rows of brick lotus petals and one of iron petals support various Buddhist attributes – alms bowl, prayer wheel etc. Chains once hung from its tip and little bells dangled from the corners of each roof. The Shijia ta, probably the oldest extant timber pagoda in China, is coloured in accordance with a usage that was widespread at that time. The outer brackets are ochre and blue, the pillars red; the inner walls were also covered with paintings.

Though the Liao sometimes erected timber buildings, as witnessed by the Yingxian pagoda, they preferred brick and used it for edifices that resembled the ancient Chinese timber towers. The pagodas on Mount Wutai, notably the Zushi ta of the Foguang si, which derived from that of the Songyue si, served the Liao as models for both style and technique. The Zushi ta is a hexagonal, two-storey pagoda, whose ground floor contains a chapel and whose upper storey, which has an engaged pillar at each corner, is a massive brick structure with five windows and, on the south side, an ornamental doorway.

One of these Liao constructions in brick is the Tianning si pagoda in Peking (early twelfth century). It is 190 feet high and has eight sides and thirteen storeys, but inside there are neither floors nor staircase. This purely decorative monument comprises three parts: (1) an octagonal base resting on a square substructure and decorated with niches, a sham balustrade and two rows of lotus petals; (2) a middle section carved with sham doors and windows framed by heavenly guardians and Bodhisattva in bold relief, whose vigorous handling is still close to their Tang models; and (3) an upper part formed by thirteen superposed roofs whose brackets imitate timber structural members. All the Liao pagodas in Hebei and Manchuria are similarly divided into three clearly marked sections.

Temples of the Song Period

Under the Northern Song Kaifeng could boast the largest Buddhist establishments of any Chinese city.

One of them, the Xiangguo si, which was patronized by the emperor and decorated with frescoes by the best religious painters of that day, was burnt down by the Jin and Yuan and subsequently rebuilt. The main buildings still extant date from the eighteenth century, but we know from documents what the monastery looked like in its heyday. It faces south and its buildings are arranged symmetrically on a south-north axis. The four main buildings on this axis are two gates, a large hall containing a Buddhist triad, and a pavilion.

The gates of the monastery had three openings. The outer gate, topped by a tower, was probably preceded by a pair of jingchuang of the type to be seen in the Lingyin si at Hangzhou. It is harder to imagine the buildings that did not lie on the median axis. There seem to have been two courtyards, each with a pagoda, an arrangement that would link the Xiangguo si plan with that of the Tang monasteries.

The only Song edifice that still preserves its original layout of A.D. 971 is the Longxing si at Zhengding (Hebei). The plan is rectangular, oriented south-north. On passing through the gate one enters a large rectangular courtyard in which stand the Drum and Bell Towers; formerly there was a hall as well. Further along the axis was the Moni dian, preceded to the east and west by two annexes. Still further north was the Ordination Terrace and behind it two symmetrical pavilions.

The Moni dian is one of the oldest extant buildings of this complex. It is square with seven bays each side (about 150 feet) and stands on a high terrace. It presents the unique feature of having a narrow vestibule or annex jutting out from each of its four sides. The roof curls up at the corners but the bracket system, which displays a great difference between the columnar and intercolumnar clusters, reveals the early date of the hall. Externally it has all the strength and elegance of Song architecture, but the interior is characterized by the confused array of supports and brackets typical of the Liao and Jin periods and bears witness to the influence of Liao motifs in the northeastern provinces.

The perfection of the Song style is illustrated by another hall, also at Zhengding – the Dacheng dian of the Xianwen miao.

After their conversion to Buddhism the Liao founded a great many religious establishments, of

Plan of the Longxing si at Zhengding, Hebei (971)

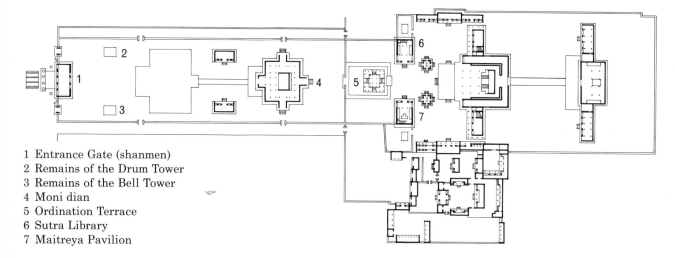

1 Entrance Gate (shanmen)
2 Remains of the Drum Tower
3 Remains of the Bell Tower
4 Moni dian
5 Ordination Terrace
6 Sutra Library
7 Maitreya Pavilion

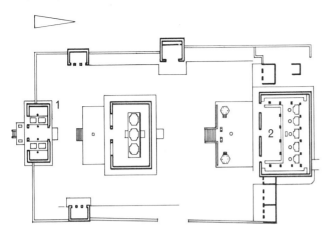

Plan of the Shanhua si at Datong (Shanxi)

1 Entrance Pavilion (shanmen)
2 Daxiongbao dian (Great Hall of the Mighty Treasure)

which the earliest derive from the Tang style. At the end of the tenth century, however, the Liao began to evolve a style of their own, first in the provinces, as witnessed by the temples on Mount Wutai. Most of the vestiges of their art date from the eleventh century, when the Song influence began to make itself felt at Datong and in the Peking region.

The Guanyin ge and the Shanmen of the Dule si at Jixian in Hebei, built in 984, date from the first period. The Guanyin ge has three storeys, only two of which can be seen from the outside. The hall has five bays on the façade and four in depth. The gallery that girdles the building above the lower roof has a balustrade. On the other hand, the extremely varied bracket clusters, each of which is admirably suited to its purpose, already prefigure the achievements of the Song period.

Shanhua si, near the South Gate of Datong (Shanxi) was also built under the Liao. In that huge monastery, which was restored under the Jin, the Daxiongbao dian dates from the Liao period. It is 130 feet (seven bays) long and 85 feet deep; its curving roof rests on multiple brackets of the Song type.

One of the few surviving examples of Taoist archi-

tecture of the Song period is the Sanqing dian, the main hall of the Xuanmiao guan temple at Suzhou (Jiangsu), built in 1179 under the Southern Song. It has nine bays on the façade and six in depth and is encircled by a verandah with a stone balustrade. The interior is divided by seven rows of ten pillars each and has a magnificent flat caisson ceiling. The double, half-hipped roof rests on an extremely varied

Bracket systems in China and Japan, from Willetts, 'Chinese Art'
a Brackets and lever arms of the upper storey of Guanyin ge (Jixian, Hebei)
b Tenjikuyō order on West Pagoda, Kaiyuan si, at Quanzhou (Fujian)
c Tenjikuyō order on Kaisandō of the Tōdaiji Temple, Nara (Japan)
d Tenjikuyō order on Nandaimon of Tōdaiji Temple

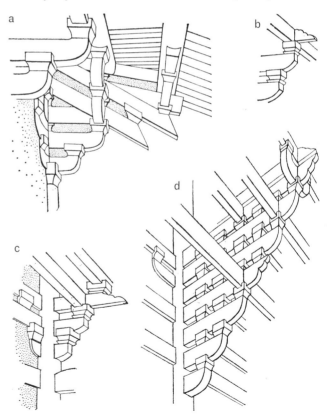

bracket system whose small members set close together prefigure the type evolved under the Ming and Qing.

The Tenjikuyō

An independent style was developed probably in Fujian on the south coast. The Japanese took it over during the last years of the twelfth century when they rebuilt the Tōdaiji Temple at Nara and gave it the name of Tenjikuyō. This style, which is poles apart from the official Song style, has two major features: the design of the bracket clusters along a single transverse axis and the slotting of the transverse arms of these clusters through the shaft of the pillar. When required by the size of the structure an intermediate support is provided between the pillars in the shape of a slanting arm (ang) reduced to its simplest form of a lever balancing two purlins.

These features are in direct contrast to the natural evolution of Chinese architecture from the Tang to the Qing, in which the brackets – both longitudinal and transverse – rest on the tops of the pillars. Yet edifices built in accordance with these two principles exist in the provinces of Fujian, Zhejiang and Guangdong. The earliest are the two granite pagodas at Quanzhou (Fujian), erected between 1228 and 1250 before the main hall of the Kaiyuan si. The vigorous style of these two five-storey, octagonal pagodas in stone is preserved in later buildings such as some halls of the Chongsheng si at Minhou xian (Fujian). The directness of the Tenjikuyō design, with its brackets arranged like an inverted stairway and a single arm projecting from the pillars, permits neither subtlety nor ornamentation. It is the beams that hold the framework together and support the roof.

The Religious Architecture of the Yuan Period

Pagodas

The basic principles of Song architecture remained valid. In Northern China brick pagodas, like that of the Zushou si at Balizhuang in the north-west suburb of Peking, still display the typical Liao features. The Balizhuang pagoda was renovated in the reign of Wan li at the end of the sixteenth century. With its octagonal plan, thirteen storeys and division into three parts – the two lower parts are adorned with sculptures – it is very close in style to the pagoda of the Tianning si in Peking, on which it was presumably modelled.

But side by side with these traditional forms appears a new type of structure, the lamaist dagoba. The earliest in Peking is the white dagoba (built of brick and painted white) of the Miaoying si erected in 1271. Thus the Indian stūpa reappeared in China in its Tibetan form introduced by the lamas of Tibet. It consists, as a rule, of a cubic basement that serves as a shrine for lamaist images; and above this, on a stepped plinth, rises a dome that swells at the summit and is pinched in lower down.

Temples

The most complete is the Yongle gong at Ruicheng (Shanxi), a Taoist temple discovered in 1949 and restored in 1959.

Building operations started in 1247 but were only finished in 1358. The magnificent frescoes that adorn the building date from that period. The five main edifices arranged on the south-north axis are the entrance gate, the Gate of the Unfathomable (Wuji men), the main hall (Sanqing dian, Hall of the Three Pure Ones), the Chungyang dian and Zhongyang dian. Originally there was another hall on the main axis and seven groups of secondary buildings to the west, but they have disappeared. All the remaining constructions date from the Yuan dynasty except for the entrance gate, which was built under the Qing.
1. The Wuji men (1294) is five bays (c. 68 feet) wide and two bays (c. 31 feet) deep. Its simple hipped roof slopes rather gently and has brackets very like the Song type.
2. The Sanqing dian, seven bays (c. 93 feet) wide and four (50 feet) deep, stands on a high base built on a terrace. Its roof is also simple and hipped. The interior of the hall is frescoed throughout and has only eight pillars to leave a maximum of free space. The

caissons of the ceiling are alternately circular and octagonal.

3. The other two buildings have half-hipped roofs. The first, the Chunyang dian, five bays (c. 67 feet) wide and three (47 feet) deep, also has fewer pillars than usual.

All four buildings have very small bracket systems, evidence of the development through which brackets lost their structural function and tended to become chiefly decorative.

The Ming and Qing

Pagodas

Few new forms were invented under the Ming but the old types were often applied on a huge scale (e.g. in the Fenzhou fu pagoda in Shanxi). The Indian dagoba continued in favour in Peking in the shape of a bottle set on a high cubic base, particularly under the Manchu emperors, who erected the White Dagoba of the Beihai (1652) and that of the Huang si (1780), both in marble.

Temples

One of the most interesting ancient temples still standing in Peking is the Zhihua si, finished in 1443. Its elongated groundplan is typical, with a series of courtyards of various sizes spread out along its axis. The main building, the Rulai dian, stands alone two storeys high in the third courtyard. The brackets that support the roof are set so close together that they give the impression of an unbroken cornice. The ceiling, now in the Nelson Gallery of Art, Kansas City, displays a certain aridity compared with earlier caisson ceilings. The religious decline that set in under the Ming is also reflected in the fact that all the edifices of the monastery buildings are small.

So few novelties appeared in the religious architecture of the Ming and Qing that I shall mention only a few buildings which diverge from tradition.

The Wuta si or Temple of the Five Pagodas in the north-west suburb of Peking was built to house the gifts brought to the emperor's court by an Indian monk at the beginning of the fifteenth century. They were 'five effigies of the Buddha in gold and a model of the Diamond Temple'; the latter was built at Bodh-Gayā, where the Buddha entered nirvana. In 1473 the emperor erected in the centre of the temple an edifice with five pagodas based on that model. It is the only part of the temple still extant – a cubic mass with five rows of recesses adorned with sculptured images of the Buddha on an ornate base decorated with floral motifs, Sanskrit characters and Buddhist emblems. The edifice has two large doorways, front and back. Inside, to right and left, two stairways lead through the stone core to the platform on which stand five tapered square towers: the one in the centre is larger than the other four. The edifice is interesting chiefly for the sculptures that adorn the outside, but its shape also must have been greatly admired, for another copy of the Bodh-Gayā temple, the dagoba of the Biyun si, was built in the sixteenth century by a rich eunuch in the north-west suburb of Peking.

The Dazhong si, Temple of the Great Bell, erected in 1733, still stands to the north of the capital. The bell, which was cast in 1406, is housed in a square pavilion that has four pillars on each side and is topped by a round tower with conical roof. The pillars and tie-beams of the upper storey form a dodecagon on which lie two rows of large beams forming squares with cut-off corners. These beams support the roof through the intermediary of short struts on which the purlins rest. The Dazhong si is a perfect example of the Chinese framework with no curved members: all circular elements lie outside it.

The great progress of brick construction under the Ming produced a type of completely vaulted building called 'wuliang dian' or 'beamless hall'. The Ying zao fa shi makes no mention of edifices of this type and none is known of before the Ming period, which leads one to infer that it was a rather late borrowing, due perhaps to the influence of lamaist Buddhism. Beamless halls of this type existed at Nanking (e.g. the big hall of the Linggu si), at Taiyan and on Mount Wutai (Shanxi), in Peking and at Suzhou (Jiansu), where the Wuliang dian in the south-west corner of the city is all that remains of the Kaiyuan monastery.

There were two methods of building these vaults. 1. The vault rises on the longitudinal axis of the edifice; the front and rear walls, which are weight-bearing, are very thick and their deep doorways and windows let in little light. Halls of this type may have one, two or three bays. 2. The vault rises on the transverse axis and comprises several successive arches. In this case the side walls are weight-bearing and therefore massive. This latter method, which admits more light, was preferred after the middle of the Ming period (e.g. at Taiyaun and on Mount Wutai).

The Wuliang dian of the Kaiyuan si in Suzhou was built in 1618 under the emperor Wan li. It has two storeys and the vault lies in the longitudinal axis. Six pillars are engaged in the south wall of each storey and under the roof there is a frieze of bracket clusters that imitate similar structures in wood. The ground floor has three arched doorways; the upper floor has five arches – the middle one frames a window, the other four are niches. Here the influence of timber construction is clear to see and the arrangement of the brick supporting members is the same as that of the pillars in halls with seven longitudinal bays.

The Temple of Confucius at Qufu

The cult of Confucius (550–479 B.C.) became, under the Han, the cult of a hero who symbolized the power and prestige of the scholar class. It spread far and wide and borrowed from the cult of Ancestors and the natural deities. For centuries every town had its temple to Confucius or temple of literature (wen-miao). The plan comprised a succession of courtyards surrounded by buildings that housed inscriptions carved on stelae and classical writings. Once a year, on the anniversary of the Sage's birthday, the local scholars and high officials met in the temple between midnight and dawn to offer the Tailao sacrifice, read liturgical essays and listen to talks. The ceremony also included music and ritual dances.

This cult was celebrated with particular pomp and ceremony in the Temple of Qufu in Shandong, where Confucius had lived and taught. Built under the Han, rebuilt, altered or enlarged under every successive dynasty, this temple dates in its present aspect from the early sixteenth century. Its rectangular walled enclosure is about 690 yards from south to north and 155 from east to west. The eleven buildings aligned on the median axis may be divided into two groups. The first, to the south, leads to the temple; it comprises stelae and edifices on each side of the median avenue. The second group, to the north, forms the temple proper, which is dominated by the main hall, the Dacheng dian, that stands on a two-storey terrace in a vast rectangular courtyard. This hall, which dates from 1724, is 85 feet high and 154 feet (nine bays) wide. Its double, half-hipped roof is covered with yellow glazed tiles. Though the building does not display any architectural novelty, it is noteworthy for its size and its rich materials: the pillars that support the lower roof are of white marble carved with dragons.

Funerary Architecture

Under the Shang (seventeenth to eleventh centuries B.C.) and Zhou (c. 100 to 256 B.C.) the vertical pit was the basic feature of tomb design. A rectangular shaft was sunk in the ground and the corpse placed at the bottom. This, with a number of variants, was the method used in the Shang tombs at Anyang (Henan), where more than 2,000 burials have been excavated.

These tombs are of three main types: 1. a simple underground pit; 2. common rectangular tombs, with a slanting corridor leading to the burial chamber, which vary in size and orientation but are arranged, as a rule, in rows and grouped in cemeteries; 3. the royal tombs with rectangular, square or cruciform pit and two corridors, one at each end, on the short sides; some have corridors on all four sides.

The largest excavated so far covers an area of 450 square yards. The consecration of these big tombs involved human and animal sacrifices. The victims were buried in holes dug in the centre of the tomb and at the four cardinal points.

This type of burial continued under the Western Zhou and the early years of the Eastern Zhou. A new form appeared during the Warring States epoch (403–221 B.C.). The coffin was placed in a chamber dug in one of the walls of the vertical pit instead of its floor. At that same time mounds began to be raised over the big tombs but the others were still grouped in cemeteries.

The chamber, which depended on the use of brick masonry, superseded the vertical pit entirely during the third century B.C.

The Qin and the Han

The introduction of the mound in China is still clothed in mystery, but under the Qin and Han it was customary for important tombs and sometimes attained a very large size. That of Qin Shi huang di (near Sian, Shânxi), which is 83 yards high and measures 530 yards by 560 at the foot, is one of the most impressive vestiges of ancient Chinese architecture. Shielded by the natural screen of the Li shan mountains, which form a broad curve behind it, 'the mound is positioned so precisely that the mountain scenery seems to have been designed in relation to it.... The manner in which history speaks of this tomb and the mention of the myriad workers (over 700,000) employed in the earth-moving operations prove that the structure (210 B.C.) struck contemporaries with a sort of holy awe, which was still further enhanced by tradition.' (V.Segalen, G. de Voisins & J.Lartigue, 'L'Art funéraire en Chine à l'époque Han', Paris 1935.)

During the Han period the essential task was to protect the body from destruction. Every possible means was employed to achieve this end–burial chambers dug in the ground or cut in the rock, mounds, and vaults to bear their weight.

The mound rose in the centre of the burial ground, whose area was proportionate to the importance of the deceased. Its orientation was suited to the lie of the land and governed by the exigencies of the fengshui system. Access to the burial ground was by the Way of the Spirits (shendao), which coincided with the median axis of the tomb. The entrance to this avenue was marked by a pair of stone piers (que), each of which leaned against a buttress pier that was smaller in size but similar in structure. The piers had a base, a rectangular shaft, a multi-storeyed entablature and a roof. They seem to have closely resembled those which stood at the entrances to cities, palaces and official buildings and which we know from representations on funerary bricks from Sichuan. The burial grounds may – like the cities – have been girdled by walls and been entered through gates resembling city gates. Twenty-three of these Later Han que are still extant. That of Liye at Zidong in Sichuan (A.D. 28) is the oldest; that of Huangshengqing at Pingyi (Feixian, Shandong) was erected in A.D. 85; the most recent is that of Gaoyi at Yaan (Sichuan), which dates from A.D. 209. These que come from Henan, Shandong and Sichuan, the provinces best known for stone engraving under the Later Han.

Within the burial ground the Way of the Spirits, which in some imperial tombs is fourfold – one towards each cardinal point – is lined by a double row of statues, stelae and piers. The mound, shaped like a truncated pyramid with rectangular base, stands on a terrace at the end of this axis and a stele engraved with the pedigree of the deceased is placed before it. Under the mound a corridor leads to one or more chambers in stone or stamped bricks. These chambers have, as a rule, corbelled vaults, sometimes circular, more seldom pointed, in accordance with a basic model widespread at that time from Manchuria to North Vietnam.

Brick tombs with corbelled vaults spread during the last years of the Western Han dynasty and gradually superseded those built of hollow bricks. The burial chambers and their annexes grew larger, their furnishings more lavish. Tombs were generally divided into two chambers, the first for the furnishings, the second for the coffin. The annexes became less important. Each arch of the vault was made of trapezoid bricks 12½ inches high with semicircular ribs in the middle of each face, recessed on one side and in relief on the other, for accurate fitting. Further, each brick had crossettes for locking together adjacent arches.

Some Han tombs have chambers built entirely of

stone. One is the big tomb at Yinan (Shandong) dating from the Later Han, which was excavated in 1954. It has three main stone chambers decorated with engraved and painted scenes from the life of a nobleman.

There are also brick tombs in which the entrance or the doorways between the chambers are of stone. In Sichuan brick tombs from the second half of the second century A.D. or the first half of the third are embellished with decorative bands of long bricks or sandstone imbricated in the walls.

The Perenniality of this Type of Burial

This type of tomb, which was apparently developed under the Han, continued during the ensuing centuries. The funerary avenues of the southern dynasties laid out in the fifth and sixth centuries were lined with statues of animals and stone piers crowned by a lion (e.g. near Nanking in Jiangsu). Under the Tang and Song the avenues grew longer and the statues more numerous, foreshadowing the tombs of the Ming emperors, the end-product of this evolution.

In important tombs the chambers had, as a rule, vaulted stone ceilings and were decorated with frescoes. An example of these aristocratic tombs of the ninth and tenth centuries is that of Wang Jian (847–918), who became emperor of Shu (Sichuan) in 907. Discovered in 1942–3, it is a huge structure covered by a mound some 15 yards high and over 85 yards in diameter. The vaulted stone chamber is almost 25 yards long. It is divided into three parts – a vestibule, a main chamber and a rear hall – separated by doors. The floor is of stone; the walls and ceiling are plastered; and the second arch is decorated with floral motifs in fresco. The coffin was placed in the main chamber on a large marble plinth supported by twelve stone warriors.

The great burial ground of the Northern Song is located south-west of Gongxian in Henan. Each tomb is surrounded by a grove of trees in accordance with a tradition that goes back to the Han and continued under the Ming and Qing. Here too each mound is reached by a Way of the Spirits lined with statues and piers.

The permanent principles of Chinese funerary ar-

chitecture – the oriented median axis, the insistence on symmetry, the vaulted chamber covered by a mound – found their proudest realization in the tombs of the Ming emperors, which were taken over by the Qing.

The Imperial Tombs of the Ming

Both in Nanking and Peking these tombs are located in a secluded spot surrounded by a vast walled park – a place of mystery and meditation.

The first Ming emperor (Hong wu) had himself buried at Nanking but after 1403 his successors, who had transferred their capital to Peking, were all buried in a vast amphitheatre girded by hills 25 miles north-west of that city. Thirteen emperors of the Ming dynasty repose in the immense necropolis, whose site was chosen by the Emperor Yong le after consulting the experts in fengshui. It occupies a plain measuring some 3 miles by 2, which rises towards the nearby mountains to the north, east and west and is crossed by a river that drains the surrounding hills.

Yong le's tomb – known as the Changling – was finished in 1415; the emperor died in 1424 and was buried there the same year. It is based on that of Hong wu at Nanking and forms the centre of the imperial necropolis. The other twelve tombs are arranged on the lower slopes of the hills that fan out around the Sacred Way. Here, as at Nanking, the general plan comprises two parts: in front the Way of the Spirits forming the median axis, further back the various buildings that make up the tomb proper.

The Way of the Spirits in the Ming Tombs (Shisan ling) at Peking

This Sacred Way leads from the Inner Red Gate to the entrance of the Changling, a distance of about 3½ miles. In 1540 it was extended another 5 furlongs from the Inner Red Gate to a white marble portico erected in that year. This portico forms a monumental gateway with five openings resting on six rectangular-section pillars. The central pillars, which are 18 feet tall, are joined about 3 feet from the top by a monolithic lintel of white marble, and above this another lintel juts out on both sides. The space between the two lintels is filled with a sculptured frieze. Similar lintels and friezes rest on the intermediate and outer pillars. The upper lintels support roofs by means of bracket clusters after the manner of timber structures. Memorial or honorific porticoes of this sort, called pailou, are not exclusive to the imperial Ming tombs. They occur here and there, built of stone or wood and varying in size and in the number of openings (three to five), straddling city streets or at the entrance to a field or temple.

The real entrance to the tombs is situated 5 furlongs beyond the portico. It is a massive gateway with three arches, a roof covered with yellow tiles and walls painted red. It was probably erected in 1425 as the official entrance to the necropolis. Some 500 yards beyond the gate stands the Stele Pavilion (1435), a square structure on a low terrace with an arched doorway on each side. Around this pavilion are four octagonal pillars in white marble, each topped by a dragon.

The Way of the Spirits continues in a slight curve lined by big stone statues of civil and military mandarins and animals such as lions, unicorns, camels, elephants and horses, arranged in pairs. Dating from 1435, they are far less vigorous and life-like than those of the Hong wu tomb at Nanking (late fourteenth century).

The long procession of statues leads northwards to a gate with three openings beyond which the Sacred Way brings us to the tomb of Yong le. This building, which is paved with stone and brick, is the focal point of the necropolis and the starting point of the Ways of the Spirits that lead to the other tombs.

The Tombs: the Changling

The plan of the Changling is a rectangle measuring roughly 360 yards by 154, flanked on one of the shorter sides by a circle about 328 yards in diameter. The rectangular part contains the buildings set aside for religious worship; the circle contains the tomb proper. After passing through the massive triple gateway that closes the tomb to the south, one enters a courtyard, about 50 yards long, at whose far end

stands another gate, the Lingen men, on a white marble terrace edged with balustrades. The Lingen men is a timber structure whose spreading roof is covered with yellow glazed tiles, and gives access to a second vast courtyard (over 160 yards long), planted with big pine trees, that leads to the Lingen dian. This hall, which closely resembles the Taihe dian of the Imperial Palace in Peking, is the most important edifice of the tomb. It stands on a three-storey, white marble terrace with balustrades at each level. It has three main stairways to the north and south and service stairways to the east and west. The timber structure is about 219 feet (nine bays) wide and 96 feet (five bays) deep. The double hipped roof rests on thirty-two pillars arranged in eight rows parallel to the long sides. This inner structure is surrounded by a colonnade of twenty-eight pillars that support the lower roof. It was used for the rites and sacrifices in the dead emperor's honour and its centre was occupied by the red wooden tablet bearing his name.

A triple gateway (the Lingqin men) gives access to a third courtyard, also planted with pine trees, which stretches for 93 yards to the foot of the minglou, or Tower of the Soul. The mound rises behind this tower; it is surrounded by a wall 10 feet thick at the top and made of rubble faced with brick outside and in. On the outside of the wall a round way is protected by battlements after the fashion of city walls.

The Dingling

The Dingling, tomb of the Emperor Wan li (1563 to 1620) and 11 furlongs from the Changling, was excavated between 1956 and 1958. Wan li was only twenty-two years old when he started building his tomb, which took six years and cost 8 million silver taels. The annals tell us that when the tomb was finished the emperor gave a reception in the burial chamber where he was interred thirty years later.

In 1956, when it was decided to excavate the tomb, the archaeologists found that they could enter the mound from the south, where part of the brick wall had caved in. They discovered a first corridor 26 feet wide, followed by a second of the same width and 437 feet long ending at a sealed wall. This wall was formed by 56 courses of bricks totalling 29 feet in height. It was topped by a roof-shaped motif covered with yellow glazed tiles. The foot of the wall was some 65 feet below the surface of the mound. A careful scrutiny showed that an opening had been cut in the wall to allow the funeral procession to pass, and subsequently sealed. The rubble seemed quite intact and revealed no trace of pillage.

On September 19, 1956, after removing some bricks from the top of this wall the archaeologists inserted an electric lamp through the opening thus formed and discovered an empty chamber. At its end was a sculptured porch with a hermetically sealed double marble door. Each leaf of the door, made of a single slab weighing 6 or 7 tons, was adorned with nine rows of knobs and an animal mask in relief. The door gave on to a vestibule that opened in turn, through an identical door, into the sacrificial chamber, which measured 105 feet by 20. Three thrones stood at the western end of this chamber in front of the door leading into the burial chamber. The emperor's throne, in the middle, was adorned with intertwined dragons and cloud motifs. The other two, reserved for the empresses, had engraved phoenixes. Five sets of altar fittings (two candlesticks, two cups and a perfume burner) in glazed pottery were set before each throne. Three jars in 'blue-and-white' porcelain still holding oil for the lamps completed the furnishings of the chamber. In the centre of each lateral wall a single-leaf door opened on to a corridor leading to a secondary chamber with a stone dais designed to carry a coffin. A door in the west wall led to a vaulted passage through which the top of the mound was reached. These annexes were meant for the two empresses in the event of their surviving Wan li. Their coffins would have been borne in through the lateral pas-sages in order not to disturb the emperor's repose. As a matter of fact, Wan li died after his two wives, and was buried between them.

The burial chamber itself was not opened until October 1957. It is a vaulted chamber measuring some 65 feet by 30 and 33 feet high, situated perpendicularly to the main axis of the tomb. The three red-lacquered coffins lay side by side on a stone dais, the emperor's in the middle, the first empress's on his left and the second empress's on his right. Each coffin had an inner and an outer casing. Objects in 'blue-and-white' porcelain and boxes in red lacquer were arranged in the space between the coffins. The boxes held jewelled weapons, head ornaments, jade pendants, garments and gold objects.

The empresses lay in their double coffins surrounded by garments and toilet articles in gold, silver and bronze, and wearing ceremonial robes and jewels. The emperor, with the crown on his head, was surrounded by silk scrolls, cups and bowls in jade enriched with gold, and ritual tablets.

The architecture of this underground palace can vie with that of the vast edifices of the Forbidden City. Besides illustrating a chapter of Chinese history it reveals an imperial art whose splendour and magnificence could hardly be imagined. The taste for the grandiose, typical of the Ming emperors, so clearly in evidence in the palaces and temples of the imperial city – it may have been due in part to the need felt by those upstarts of lowly origin to prove their worth in the face of a millenary tradition – is no less obvious here. The ensemble of the Ming tombs in Peking is more complete than the mausoleum of Hong wu at Nanking, and consequently more famous. But it derives from the latter and though perhaps more magnificent, it has not the same sober grandeur.

153

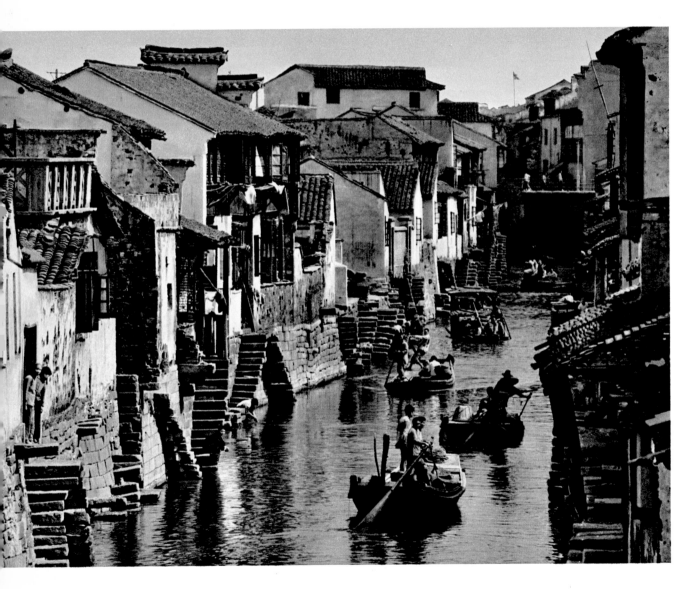

The Ou Garden at Suzhou (Jiangsu)
Groundplan 1:75

This extensive home of a man of letters, with gardens to the east and west, is surrounded on the east, south and north by a small stream

1 Garden
2 Rockery
3 Courtyard
4 Main entrance
5 Reception room
6 Library
7 Large reception room
8 Sedan-chair depot
9 Kiosk
10 Open pavilion

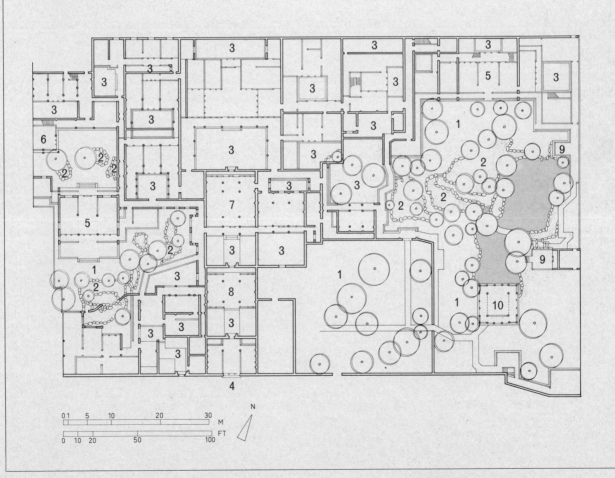

0 1   5   10   20   30
                                         M
0 10 20   50   100
                                         FT

N

An Official's Residence at Xinning xian, Hunan: Groundplan 1:300

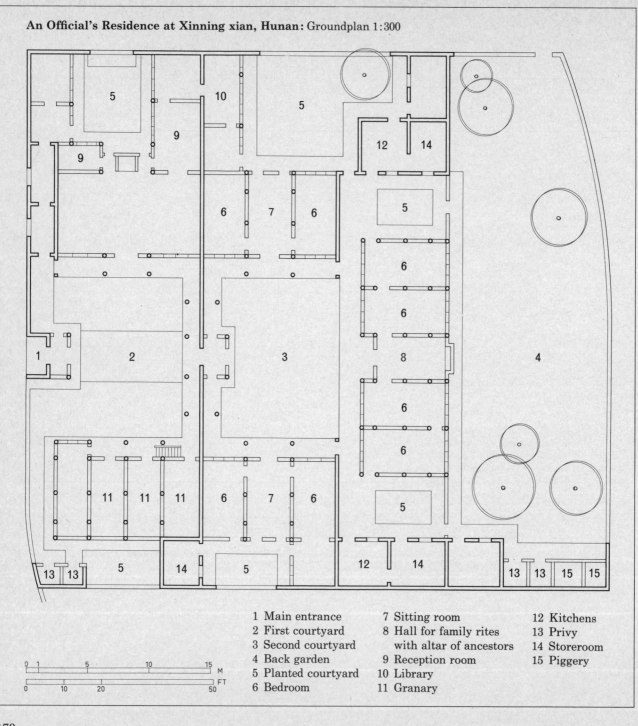

1 Main entrance
2 First courtyard
3 Second courtyard
4 Back garden
5 Planted courtyard
6 Bedroom
7 Sitting room
8 Hall for family rites
  with altar of ancestors
9 Reception room
10 Library
11 Granary
12 Kitchens
13 Privy
14 Storeroom
15 Piggery

5. Houses and Gardens

The Chinese Dwelling House

The house is a refuge from the outside world, the smallest unit of humanized space. In China it was felt to be profoundly personal, contrasting, in its order and integration, with a still untamed nature.

The Han Period
(third century B.C. to third century A.D.)

The building boom of the time resulted in a definitive crystallization of the traditional features of the Chinese dwelling house. It is possible, however, that the importance of this fact is overestimated owing to the mass of documentation provided by funeral furnishings. Nor should we forget that the Han profited by older traditions and innovations of which not a trace exists today.

A difference must be drawn between small dwellings and important residences of the Han period.

1. Small Dwellings
a) Square or rectangular houses with timber framework in the south (models found in tombs at Changsha, Hunan, and in Sichuan), with brick walls in the Yellow River valley. The saddle roof had narrow eaves and was usually covered with tiles but sometimes with clay.
b) L-shaped dwellings of one or two storeys built round a courtyard with timber superstructure and roof as in the foregoing category. The upper storey, where it existed, housed the owner and was reached by an outside staircase; livestock was kept on the ground floor.
c) Buildings round a courtyard.
d) Buildings arranged in two parallel rows separated by a courtyard. The building in front, which was the more important, had two storeys and the middle of the upper section was elevated to form a watchtower.

2. Large Dwellings
The engraved stones found in burial chambers such as the Wuliangzi tomb in Shandong show a courtyard surrounded by buildings on all four sides. This was typical of upper-class dwellings. Family life

Tombal pottery model of a Western Han house found near Canton in 1956 (Historical Museum, Peking)

tors were also kept. That was the most honourable side and the family fortunes dwelt there. The room to the north-east was often used for storing provisions. Behind this building rich families had pleasure grounds with summerhouses and artificial lakes.

This traditional house, the centre of family life and devotions, was shielded from prying eyes by walls or hedges. Its only door to the outside world was often located to one side and almost hidden.

The Rules Governing the Building of the House

Building a house has always been considered as an important act that could exert a strong influence on the future of those destined to live in it. For this influence to be beneficial it was considered essential to choose a plot, a site, an orientation and a plan that conformed with the demands of geomancy and to begin operations on a propitious day. A start was not

developed in a closed space and the home presented a blind front to the outside world. The inner courtyard was called 'the well of heaven' (tianjing). 'The term', as Prof. R. Stein says, 'derives from the fact that the rainwater streaming from the surrounding roofs collects in its centre in a sort of pool or quagmire. What is more, the jing character is used to designate an arrangement of space in a sort of magic square with eight compartments and a ninth in the centre, a shape identical with the mingtang. The atrium, which was the centre of the Roman house, is extraordinarily like the centre of the Chinese house.'

The basic type of Chinese domestic architecture during the ensuing periods continued to be the house built round a courtyard. The dwellings of princely families might have several courtyards but the main entrance always faced south and the remotest building was the main hall, which was reached by a row of steps and was divided into three parts: the reception room in the middle, flanked on right and left by two smaller living rooms. The head of the family occupied the south-east corner, where the tablets of the ances-

End tile, Han dynasty (Musée Guimet, Paris)

made until all the sacrifices had been offered. The first job was to level the ground, which was rammed with wooden beetles or a big stone that was thrown with the help of a rope and served to level the ground and ram it at the same time. Then the foundations were laid in rough stones or bricks and built up to a foot above the ground except at the points where the pillars were to stand, which were left hollow. Once the pillars were set in place, filling in the walls was the last job before fitting the roof.

Dwellings were governed not only by the rules of fengshui but also by the laws promulgated by each dynasty, which aimed at preserving the social hierarchy on which the Chinese social system was based. The Tang regulations ordered that 'below (the rank of) kings and dukes houses shall have neither double brackets nor decorations (on the beams). Below officials of the third grade the main hall shall not have more than five bays...' This hierarchy was fixed down to officials of the sixth or seventh grade, that is down to the common people, whose main building was not to exceed three bays and the main door not more than one bay. Moreover, private houses were not to have upper storeys from which one could see into other people's homes. These limitations were adopted by subsequent dynasties. The size of an official's reception room depended on his grade right and the houses of the common people at the beginning of the Ming period were not allowed to have either brackets or painted decorations. There was also a hierarchy concerning the size of buildings based on the number of bays, which ranged from eleven for the most respectable edifices to three for the annexes of large ensembles, the reception rooms of minor officials and the dwellings of the common people.

Song Innovations

This traditional type of house continued in use with few changes from about the beginning of our era to the Qing dynasty and the only innovations concerned details.

In the Song period the groundplan was amended by linking two or three parallel buildings with a gallery or a hall erected on the median axis. Other modifications concern the doors and windows. The latter, which since the Six Dynasties period had been strengthened with robust bars, were transformed under the Song by latticework in the upper half and solid panels below, which could be opened or shut. At the same time doors with an openwork lozenge pattern in the upper part came to be widely used.

Dwelling House Types under the Ming and Qing

This is the period we know best thanks to the abundant documentation and the many examples still extant. I shall give a brief account of the typically 'Han' variants and leave aside those characteristic of the ethnic minorities.
1. Round houses in Inner Mongolia and the neighbouring regions of China. This type of mud house derived from the Mongol tent. Initially the roof was supported by a central pillar; later the walls were strengthened for the same purpose. The door was generally on the south and there were two small windows.
2. Rectangular houses oriented north-south: half-underground in the western region of Inner Mongolia, with thatched roof covered with dry mud; built on piles among the ethnic minorities of South-Western China; also the typical dwelling of small artisans and poor peasants in Northern and Central China. In these last the entrance was on the south side, the walls were of mud or brick, and the lean-to or saddle roof was covered with tiles or thatch.
3. Rectangular houses oriented east-west, the commonest type for small dwellings. One of the long sides faced south to catch as much sun as possible for protection against the winter cold. Doors and windows opened on the south side. Variations concern size, materials (timber, mud, brick, stone, bamboo) and the shape of the roof.

These houses ranged in size from one to seven bays; the largest could lodge as many as three families. Three-bay houses were commonest and their shape and materials differed most from one region to another. In Hebei, for instance, the base of the walls was of stone and the upper part of mud; the saddle roof had narrow eaves. The living-room was in the middle, flanked on each side by a smaller room occupied by the kang, which was set against the south window. This kang, typical of the houses of Northern China, was a bed made of rammed earth faced with brick round the sides and overlaid with padded coverlets. Conduits under the kang provided an evenly distributed heat.

4. L-shaped houses. Already used in the days of the Eastern Han. Two variants appear under the Ming and Qing – one shut in by walls; the other unfenced, derived from the three-bay house.

5. Courtyards with buildings of one or two storeys on three sides, common in the villages and small towns of Southern China. In some cases the north, or main, wing alone had an upper floor.

6. Courtyards with buildings on all four sides. The homesteads of rich peasants, merchants and the governing class. The two chief features were the enclosed layout and the symmetrical arrangement of the buildings.

– Ground floor only: the main gateway was either on the median axis (in the provinces south of the River Huai and the north-east region) or in the south-east, north-east or north-west corner (in the Peking region and the provinces of Shandong, Shanxi, Henan and Shânxi);

– multi-storey, usually two but sometimes as many as four or five in Fujian, Guangdong and Guangxi.

7. Homesteads that combined the courtyard with buildings on three sides and that with buildings on all four sides. This type, which was common in the south, might have one or more storeys.

8. Cave-dwellings, common in Henan, Shanxi, Shânxi and Gansu, namely loess regions where timber is scarce and rainfall scanty. At the beginning of the Qing period cave-dwellings existed only in Shanxi; by the end of the dynasty they had become the normal type of dwelling for the poor peasants of the four provinces in the western basin of the Yellow River. They were either completely troglodytic, with a narrow façade and extending in depth, or semi-troglodytic, with brick walls and an almost flat roof covered with mud or with tiles laid on mud. These caves, which had the advantage of being easy to heat in winter and always cool in summer, were sometimes strengthened with an inner stone vaulting.

Summing up, the majority of common people's homes seem to have been either rectangular (with from one to three bays), L-shaped or troglodytic. The upper classes, instead, built rectangular houses (with more than three bays from east to west) or homesteads with three or four buildings round a courtyard – a layout capable of being expanded.

Most of these dwellings faced south but the lie of the land might entail a different orientation. The shape of the roof varied from one region to another. Gabled roofs were current in the provinces with heavy rainfall; pent, flat or round roofs in the regions where it seldom rains. The flat roof, whether mud-covered or thatched, was very common among the poorer classes in Northern China; its slightly rounded shape recalled the hood of a cart. It was cheaper than a tiled roof and its solidity, thickness and insulating properties made it very suitable for cold climates.

The Interior Arrangement of Large Residences under the Ming and Qing

Many wealthy families occupied the same residence for four, five or even six generations. The parents and grandparents lived in the central building that faced south, the children in the buildings on each side. Servants were housed in the annexes off the median axis.

The Arrangement of Upper-Class Homes in the Peking Region with Courtyard Closed on all Four Sides

The main gate (da men) was very often off the median axis, a little to the south-east. It had two leaves lacquered red and an outer threshold in decorated stone. The porter's lodge, servants' quarters and other annexes were located on the axis of the gate. Behind the portal was the wall of the genii (yingbi or zhaobi), a sort of screen designed to keep out evil spirits which, it was commonly believed, could only move in a straight line. Walls of the genii, which were found in private houses, palaces and temples, were usually embellished with terracotta reliefs; in buildings of some importance these were glazed and painted. The most famous and impressive is the Wall of the Nine Dragons in the Beihai in Peking. It is faced with green, yellow, blue and aubergine bricks, and protected the entrance to a temple that has disappeared.

After this protective screen the visitor passed through another door into the first courtyard, which was adorned with rockeries and flowering plants in troughs. The reception room (da ting) opened on to this courtyard; on the right was the master's library, on the left his rest room. This first building was the public part of the dwelling, beyond which, in principle, no man except members of the family and certain servants could penetrate. Where there were three courtyards the second was reserved for the living quarters of the family; it was surrounded by galleries on to which their windows opened and which enabled the inmates to pass from one room to another under cover.

The apartments on the right and left (xiang) were set aside for concubines, married sons and close relatives. At the far end of the courtyard stood a building, usually containing five rooms, that was occupied by the master of the house and his first wife. The room in the middle held the altar of the ancestors; the small rooms at each end were storerooms. Behind this second ensemble a third courtyard with a well comprised the kitchen and the maidservants' quarters. When this typical plan was expanded, a second reception room for important guests was built on a courtyard specially designed for that purpose.

The Ming Houses of Huizhou in South-East Anhui

In this region there are houses that were built between the end of the fifteenth century and the seventeenth. They are situated in small towns or in the open country and belonged to merchants enriched by the salt monopoly in the sixteenth century. Usually of two storeys, they open towards the south and have an east-west courtyard in which there is frequently a pond. The rooms on the front (annexes and store-rooms) and sides are lower than the rear hall, which contained the main living quarters. This latter has two storeys: upstairs the ancestors' room is flanked on each side by a bedroom; the same arrangement occurs on the ground floor round the reception room. The kitchens are located behind this main room, but may also occupy a small brick annex. The outer walls of dwelling houses vary in thickness from 11 to 13 inches; they are made of whitewashed brick and are usually quite high.

The Chinese homestead, with its buildings, commons and courtyards enclosed by grey brick walls, is a symbol of security, of the respect for social and family order. It is complemented by gardens that open on the world of nature, freedom and caprice and harmonize ideally with the landscape.

Gardens

The Chinese Idea of the Garden

A garden is a closed, infinitely malleable world that embodies the age-old dream of the microcosm. Failing to meet nature face to face, as they would have liked to do, the Chinese intelligentsia recreated it on a smaller scale. For this reason the art of gardening is one of the most typical manifestations of Chinese architectural genius.

Far from slavishly imitating nature, the Chinese garden is a pure product of the imagination. Its value lies essentially in the suggestions it makes, the ideas it expresses and the charm it distils. This charm is due less to the layout of the garden and the elements of which it is composed than to its natural rhythm, the interplay of light and shade, the slow motion of water, the thousand pulsations that reveal an intimate contact with untamed nature.

These old gardens also satisfy a number of peculiar criteria:
1. The choice of the site tends to recover, as in landscape painting, the natural motivation and recreate a nature that is more ideal and exemplary than nature herself – a sort of poetic quintessence of nature.
2. The various elements that make up a Chinese garden give the impression, on the scale of the micro-

Shen Zhou (1427–1509): spring landscape, dating from 1491
(Freer Gallery of Art, Washington)

cosm, of a stroll in the country. The unfettered caprice of that stroll is one of the essential themes of the garden and so governs its layout. In fact, one can never get a complete idea of it from a single viewpoint. It consists of a succession of more or less isolated sections that must be discovered and enjoyed by degrees.

The stroller follows the paths through a composition that never shows itself in its entirely and so preserves the charm of the mysterious. He discovers the garden just as one discovers a painting when one unwinds the scroll, in keeping with a temporal dimension that is a peculiar quality of all Chinese art.

The Chinese garden is not only a spiritual itinerary; it is also a refuge designed for leisure, conversation, meditation and the refined pleasure involved in drinking wine, reciting poems, examining a work of art. Closely linked with the home, a garden is the place to spend unguarded moments, a wonderland that offers aesthetic enjoyment of a stone, a tree or a flower.

Chinese gardens vary enormously with the climate, the vegetation, the site. Hence a garden in Suzhou (Jiangsu) cannot resemble one in Peking, even if both are designed along the same principles. A distinction must also be drawn between urban and country gardens. In China urban gardens occupied a far greater area and were far more developed than in the west. These walled gardens formed an extension of the dwelling; they contained summerhouses, libraries and small rooms for drinking tea, making music or studying. These pavilions and verandahs, while affording a certain amount of shelter and isolation, gave the impression of being in the open air surrounded by a dream landscape.

This how a certain Pan En describes his garden in Shanghai: 'To the west of my house there used to be a vegetable garden, fields and trees. In the year 1559, when I finished my work in the Office of Cults in Peking, being faced with a certain period of leisure I gathered a number of rocks and asked some workmen to arrange them to my liking. I dug a pool, built a pavilion and planted bamboos.... I continued building this garden for twenty years.... There was also a doorway somewhere on the west on which one could read this inscription: "Beauty enters by degrees."'

Another type of garden dear to the Chinese surrounded study pavilions in the mountains, where poets, philosophers and artists used to be fond of taking refuge amid trees, bamboos and flowers. A great many poems and paintings illustrate this unpretentious type of garden, which was an oasis of silence at the vague confines of nature and our inner world:

'The herb path covered with red moss,
The mountain window filled with pale blue sky...
My friend, I envy you your wine, under the flowers,
And all those butterflies that flutter in your dreams.'
                                            Qian Qi (8th century)

There the recluse had the dual privilege of communing with nature and creating a private world of his own in miniature.

The Elements of the Garden

What counts most in a garden, as in a landscape painting, is shanshui (mountains and streams); but trees, flowers and architectural motifs are also important elements. Mountains, buildings and plantations provide relief and the effects of light and shade. Paths and streams give the composition rhythm, movement and variety in a rippling play of supple lines. All these elements make a garden a self-contained little world from which are banished all symmetry and order and every slightest thing that might give an impression of rigidity.

Mountains and Streams

For the Chinese water is what makes a garden live, and the choice of a site is conditioned by the existence of water points. The ancient gardens of Suzhou (Jiangsu) and the Yuanming yuan in Hebei owed their beauty to their abundant water supply. The poetry of water, of pools that reflect lights and shadows, gives a garden its peculiar magic. It takes hold of all too solid objects and dissolves them in its imperceptible pulsation. In the closed space of a Chinese garden, the sinuous streams and curving lakes are so designed that one can never see where they terminate.

The 'mountains' are the most original and most specifically Chinese element of these gardens. Here rockeries are the expression of a very old cultural tradition and a deeply felt interest in the mineral world. The Chinese have always considered mountains and oddly shaped rocks as the loftiest symbols of nature's creative powers, which made them, no less than human beings, just what they are. Folklore is full of haunted rocks in wild places. It was to satisfy this taste for rockeries that stones of peculiar shape or associated with an ancient legend were transplanted to urban gardens.

The capacity for visualizing a whole mountain in a single rock seems to have matured under the Tang. The rockeries in the gardens of the Six Dynasties had probably been piles of stones designed to represent a mountain. The Tang cognoscenti replaced those piles by a single monumental rock that did not aim at being a naturalistic representation of a mountain but its ideal, symbolic image. Song writers displayed a lively taste for rocks whose shape, structure or colour made them unusual or rare. Rocks formed so ingeniously by nature were highly prized playthings. Many books were written at that time about rare rocks that were worth enormous prices. The first, Yu lin shi pu (Catalogue of Rocks of the Forest of the Clouds), was written early in the twelfth century by Du Wan, a collector who sums up the use of rocks in these words: 'The objects that constitute the purest quintessence of Heaven and Earth are incorporated in rocks; they pierce the earth and assume strange shapes.... Big ones deserve to be arranged in a house or garden, small ones may be placed on stands or tables.' A stone, as a mountain or microcosm, inspired a man with noble thoughts, patience, stability and led him to seek seclusion and the wise contemplation of nature.

Some rocks of this kind came from Shanxi, others from Guangdong; the most highly prized were blocks of limestone moulded by the waters of Lake Taihu or some other lake in Southern China. The finest were viewed as nature's masterpieces and set on pedestals, reproduced in paintings and celebrated in poems. The value of a stone was determined first and foremost by nature's handiwork, but man's intervention was not debarred. Indeed, it was an indispensable adjunct in the art of gardening. Thus, one of the best locations for a mountain was the middle of a lake, as in the Shizi lin at Suzhou. Another good position for a rock was before a white wall: the white background performed the same function as the sheet of paper on which rocks are painted. A rock was often accompanied by a pine tree or a bamboo. Symmetrical arrangement was scrupulously avoided: a 'natural' effect was always sought. Compositions of this type attained the greatest variety and fancy at the end of the Ming period. At that time artists succeeded in giving their artificial mountains a weightlessness which made them seem to rise in the empty air.

Trees and Flowers

For the Chinese flowers are not an indispensable element of a garden. They are appreciated for their symbolic significance more than for their ornamental value. The three most highly prized plants are perhaps the plum tree, whose white flowers usher in the spring, the bamboo and the pine. They are called the 'three friends' of the cold season. For men of letters the bamboo, a miraculous combination of suppleness

Shen Zhou: The Gardeners, page from a sketchbook (William Rockhill Nelson Gallery of Art, Kansas City)

and strength, is a symbol of friendship and long life. It is the wisest of plants because it bends its head before the storm and straightens up again when it is past. Bamboos occupy a privileged position in all Chinese gardens, at least south of the Yellow River.

The pine is the supreme symbol of longevity not only because its foliage is always green but also because of the transformations it undergoes during its long life. In a garden the tortured branches of a pine harmonize with the oddly shaped rocks from which it is inseparable. Hoary pine trees and time-worn stones are tokens of long life and numerous posterity, but also of silence and solitude. As Li Liweng wrote at the end of the Ming period, 'to sit in a garden with peach trees, flowers and willows but without a single pine is like sitting in the midst of women and children without a venerable man to look at by one's side.'

Longevity, as expressed by their gnarled and knotty branches, is a quality shared by the sacred trees that surround tombs and temples and those that accompany rocks in parks and gardens – enclosures where one can meditate or meet one's friends.

The peach tree is also a symbol of longevity for it wards off evil spirits. It is worth noting that fruit trees are never planted in Chinese gardens for utilitarian purposes. The orchard and the vegetable garden so dear to classical antiquity and the Muslim world are poles apart from the idea on which the gardens of Chinese men of letters are based.

Innumerable other species are found in the various regions: species similar to the acacia, the catalpa in the north, cypresses and conifers.

The flowers vary with the seasons, ranging from the orchid with its feminine charm to the autumnal chrysanthemum and the luscious summer peony; they are always planted in large clumps. Last, but not least, in July the water lily lends ineffable beauty to lakes and pools; in that matchless beauty Chinese literati saw purity and peace.

The Architectural Elements of the Garden

The Chinese speak of 'building' a garden, not 'planting' one. This is clear proof of the close link between

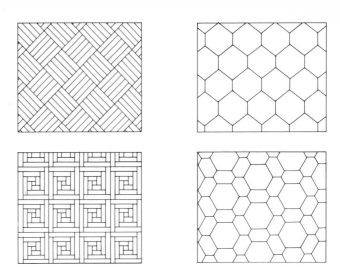

Motifs for the pavement of a garden path: mosaics in brick or brick and rubble

garden and architecture, the importance of doorways and decorative windows cut in the walls, of pavilions, bridges and galleries – the basic elements that frame and divide the landscape.

The open galleries are an invitation to walk or rest. Connecting, as they do, buildings and the different parts of the garden, they emphasize the flat sheets of water and the steep hillsides. The vistas afforded by their curving course give the composition unity and picturesqueness. No Chinese garden would be complete without an open gallery with balustrades adorned with an infinite variety of geometrical motifs.

Another organic element is the wall, which is intimately related to the scenery and the lie of the land. Rarely straight, it usually bends to follow the contours and the impression it gives is one of flexibility and sculptural relief rather than of rigidity and linearity. Its white plaster facing provides a background on which trees and rocks cast their shadows. This white expanse is broken by ornamental openings of every shape and form, through which one enjoys vistas whose charm lies in their unexpectedness. The Chinese mentality delights in the accidental and unforeseen; in gardens as in landscape paintings it insists on interruptions and ellipses. 'When the Ancients painted plum trees or bamboos, they only let us see a single branch projecting from behind a wall and grasped its character completely from that uncommon angle. Had they painted the whole tree, with all its branches, they would have sunk into the insipidity of the commonplace.' These revealing words by Shen Hao at the beginning of the Qing period may be applied to the effects obtained by opening a window or a doorway in the wall, through which one glimpses the fragmentary, asymmetric composition of a clump of bamboo and a perforated rock. Thus divorced from its context, the object is stripped of its trite materiality.

Bridges of stone or timber, arched or flat, form an irregular path which is the natural complement to the linear interplay of open pavilions and zig-zag walks. At times, in the pursuit of wildness and rusticity, where the water is not too deep the bridge is replaced by a causeway of large flat stones. Garden paths are paved with a combination of stone slabs, pebbles, broken tiles and fragments of brick forming a mosaic whose patterns and colours vary endlessly. As a rule the patterns are geometric (polygons or quatrefoils) and match those that adorn the balustrades. The more realistic designs (deer, birds, fishes) in some nineteenth-century gardens were thought vulgar.

Gardens and Painting

The art of gardening follows landscape painting and endeavours to attain the same ideal. One might even say that the garden, as a place for contemplation and solitude and the product of an art at once intimate, humane and sophisticated, is a landscape painting in three dimensions. It is not surprising therefore that garden planners were strongly influenced by painters and that in the past gardening was a branch of painting. Conversely, the love of rocks displayed by some Song, Yuan and Ming painters allured garden lovers right up to the end of the nineteenth century.

Garden designers, like painters, were interested first and foremost in rhythm. A garden is a spot where man's vitality and nature's clash and harmonize; it is the triumph of man's effort to find his place in the universe. As such it sets a trap for nature: when it seems utterly natural it attains the unattainable. In gardening, as in landscape painting, rhythm is achieved by alternating full and empty spaces. White walls replace the clouds, mists and vapours of a painting – islands of whiteness amid the inky black of the mountains. Those pale areas enable the imagination to relay the eye, and consummate the union of reality and illusion, which in China is still the ideal of both the painter's and the gardener's art. That is what Shen Fu (b. 1763), who wrote 'Six Stories in the Fickle Course of Time', called 'opening dense spaces by rendering reality unreal.' The splendid pages he devoted to the art of gardening are more precious than any treatise on the subject because they are the fruit of experience and invention. He says: 'In planning a garden with architectures, hills, rockeries and flowers success depends not only on the complexity of the design, the vastness of the area or the number of rocks. Its secret lies in these few principles: create small closed spaces in the midst of large areas; give the illusion of vastness even where space is restricted; give empty spaces density by making unreality manifest; alternate the mysterious and the obvious, facile approaches and remote retreats.... Giving empty spaces density by making unreality manifest may consist, for instance, after rounding a hill that seemed definitively to block the way in contriving a sudden vista of a vast open horizon...'

The Evolution of the Private Garden

From the Han to the Tang

The idea of representing a natural site complete on a miniature scale dates from the Han period and is linked apparently with religious, mystic and traditional concepts that originated with the Taoists and spread to other circles. It was then that zoological, botanical and pleasure gardens were first laid out.

The evolution of the art of gardening owes much to the retreats where poets and Taoist hermits sought communion with nature. But Buddhist monasteries, which were located as a rule in spots of great beauty, also helped to penetrate the mysteries of the universe. This was more in evidence after the rise of the Chan sect.

The taste for gardens spread and was diversified during the Tang period with the development of large estates known variously as 'suburban villas' or 'country places', which included pleasure grounds. We know of some of these villas from poetical descriptions or because they belonged to famous people. The villa of Wang-chuan (at Lantian in Shânxi) was celebrated by its owner, the poet and landscape painter Wang Wei (699–759), who retired there towards the end of his life to write and paint.

'Sitting alone and apart amidst the bamboos,
I play the zither and sing out loud;
In the deep forest where men have forgotten me,
Only a moonbeam comes to bring me light.'

Another famous villa of the Tang period, at Pingquan near Luoyang (Henan), belonged to the great minister Li Deyu (787–850), who was also a poet and collected rare perennials, a great many varieties of which were obtained from wild flowers at that time by selection and grafting. The grounds that surrounded the house seem to have been half rockery, half botanical garden. The proprietor, a great connoisseur of stones, planted rocks streaked with flashing crystals in his retreat, which contained a pool, a brook and many dwarf trees. This garden was part of an estate of some 500 acres situated on a mountainside in a landscape that offered an infinite variety of natural prospects.

The grand gardens of the governing class and the simpler ones of the literati paved the way for the art of gardening that flourished under the Song.

The Song

The Song garden, which derived from the Tang villa, very soon adopted a formula in which house and garden were closely linked. Extensive rural gardens did not disappear, but men of letters began to prefer small town gardens designed to harmonize with their houses. Rockeries and artificial mountains became increasingly important features, side by side with adaptation to the lie of the land, the natural site and the seasons of the year. These features were also typical of Ming and Qing gardens.

The Ming and Qing

During this period, which may be termed the golden age of the private garden, the most creative centres were Peking in the north and Zangzhou, Nanking, Suzhou and Hangzhou in the south.

Those that still exist give only a vague idea of the art of gardening in ancient China. But in some cities we can sense the atmosphere and the spirit that presided over their creation. One is Suzhou, which continued to be a haven for writers and artists until the end of the nineteenth century. Its period of greatest influence was under the Ming dynasty, when many leading poets and painters lived there.

The oldest of the gardens preserved or restored in Suzhou is probably the Shizi lin (the Lion's Covert), laid out by a monk about 1342. It is famous for its rockery. Some of the rocks are set on a hillock amid knotty old pines; others are arranged in a very simple pictorial composition; others still are mirrored in the waters of a pool. Unfortunately, this garden has undergone a great many restorations, with the result that the importance of the rockery is exaggerated and there is a certain imbalance between rocks, trees and buildings.

Another splendid garden in the Ming tradition in Suzhou is the Liu yuan, laid out in the sixteenth century round a lake that constitutes its major motif and occupies over half its area. In the nineteenth century it was bought by a family who enlarged it and endeavoured to recapture the spirit that animated gardens in the past. The prospects are varied in the extreme. Paths meander amid rockeries and isolated stones; bamboo groves alternate with courtyards; windows frame glimpses of banana leaves silhouetted against a white wall.

The Wangshi yuan in the south part of the town is far smaller, yet it succeeds in seeming deep, impenetrable, mysterious. There also the central motif is a lake surrounded by huge blocks of stone, ancient trees, bridges and galleries. One of its charms is the unity, sobriety and perfect harmony of its layout. Since it was lived in until 1949, one still feels, more than in any other garden in Suzhou, the presence of man's hand and love.

Early in the eighteenth century Yangzhou ousted Suzhou from the place it had occupied until the fall of the Ming dynasty. There the great painter Shi Tao gained a reputation as a garden architect and designed the rockeries for two ensembles now destroyed and for most of the gardens in Yangzhou.

The finest Chinese gardens were to be found in the south, but under the Qing dynasty Peking had no lack of splendid gardens.

The Imperial Parks

As a rule the residences of the Chinese emperors were of two sorts – an official residence in the capital and a country seat in the mountains or on the lakeside nearby. Those pleasure grounds contained the rarest trees and flowers and their layout gave fancy a free reign. In the history of the Han dynasty one reads of two lakes, Tangzhong and Taiyi north of Changan. The Jiantai Palace stood in the centre of the latter. In its grounds the Emperor Wu cultivated such recently imported plants as the walnut, pomegranate, cinnamon and grape vine. Plants and animals brought from all over the empire confirmed the Son of Heaven's power over his universal domain.

Under the Tang the imperial gardens stretched as far south as the North Wall of Changan. This forbidden park (Jinyuan) was bordered on the east and north by the rivers Ba and Wei; on the west it comprised part of the Changan of the Han. It contained kiosks, towers, terraces, pavilions, palaces and lakes.

In more recent times the Ming and Qing emperors built parks and summer residences in Peking and its suburbs, of which some traces still exist.

The Lake Parks West of the Imperial Palace

During the Jin period a long sheet of water was dug on the site where the emperor wanted to lay out pleasure grounds. The Yuan enlarged this lake and

the surrounding park. In the fifteenth century the Nanhai was opened and the three lakes Behai, Zhonghai and Nanhai were given their final form. The Manchu emperors left not a trace of the structures erected in this park by the Mongols or the early Ming. Work continued under Kang xi and Qian long and was completed by the Dowager Empress Ci xi (Ts'eu-hi). The many Qing edifices served as temples, theatres, libraries, dwellings, reception rooms, pavilions for writing poetry, turrets, rockeries.

The Summer Palaces

Whereas the Ming emperors' summer palaces were situated to the south of Peking, all those built during the seventeenth and eighteenth centuries were erected a few miles north-west of the city. Today very little is left of those imposing constructions.

The Yuanming yuan (The Garden of Perfect Clarity) was a vast enclosure that must have measured originally at least 125 miles round. Under the Qing dynasty a number of palaces and pavilions surrounded by gardens were built there. The oldest section, founded by Kang xi, was called Changchun yuan (the Garden of Glorious Spring). In 1709 the same emperor gave another piece of land to his son, the future Yong zheng (1723–35). Further additions were made in the reign of Qian long, who was not content to build Chinese pavilions but called in the Jesuits who worked at his court – particularly Brother Castiglione and Father Benoist – to erect a group of European-style palaces surrounded by vast gardens embellished with fountains. All that remains of these buildings, which were modelled on those of Borromini, Guardini and Bibiena, are a few forlorn ruins in the open country. In 1751 Qian long built the Changchun yuan to the east of the Yuanming yuan. Its buildings comprised audience halls and the emperor's private apartments. There Qian long spent most of the year, only occupying the Imperial Palace in Peking during the winter months. In the Changchun yuan he had copies made of southern landscapes he was particularly fond of and famous gardens such as the Shizi lin.

At the end of the nineteenth century, when the Chinese court wanted to restore at least some part of the ruined palaces, it concentrated its efforts on the Wanshou shan, where Qian long's mother had lived. Yihu yuan was the name given this new summer palace, most of whose buildings date from 1903. Before being turned into a public park, it was the favourite residence of the Dowager Empress Ci xi.

The Yihe yuan (the Garden of Peace and Harmony) cannot bear comparison with the summer palaces of the eighteenth century. The splendid lake that occupies three quarters of its area cannot make one forget the stiffness, bad taste and excessive decoration of the gatehouses, palaces and galleries, which

The Yuanming yuan (Garden of Perfect Clarity) north-east of the Summer Palace (Bibliothèque nationale, Paris)

Pavilion in a lake, Yuanming yuan (Bibliothèque nationale, Paris)

were erected when the decadence of imperial art was in full swing.

Conclusion

The Chinese art of gardening that produced the Japanese gardens also influenced – though far more superficially – the picturesque gardens of eighteenth-century Europe. The first English gardens in the new style, designed between 1720 and 1730, were inspired directly and deliberately by Chinese motifs, but they failed to grasp their spirit. This spirit seems, indeed, so closely linked with Chinese ideas that it evades a first contact. Chinese men of letters, in their reaction against a rigid hierarchy whose rites and rules were based exclusively on convention, found an escape from formalism and routine in their gardens. A garden represented freedom organized by man for his own pleasure and the ideal insertion in the urban microcosm of a private territory for each family cell: a fragment of recreated and idealized nature. Like all retreats – tomb, house, hermitage or monastery – this refuge is a haven of peace and quiet. Moreover, like all manifestations of Chinese architecture, it bears the stamp of transience. Thus the garden, a fragile impermanent creation, possesses a latent dynamic that is one of its essential qualities. In architecture this dynamic expresses itself in flexible timber structures, in wavering lines, in the prevalence of sharp angles. Here it is revealed in curves and zig-zags, in the interplay of light and shade.

Chinese architecture, already timeless through its loyalty to a programme and its surrender to official requirements, in private buildings is freer still from the bonds of time owing to the restricted means at its disposal.

Chronological Table

Dynasty	Monuments	Date	Location
Shang (17th–11th cent. B.C.)	traces at Zhengzhou	c. 16th–14th cent. B.C.	Henan
	traces at Anyang	14th–11th cent. B.C.	Henan-
Zhou & Warring States (1028–221 B.C.)	traces at Houma	6th–5th cent. B.C.	Shânxi
	traces at Linzi	6th–5th cent. B.C.	Shandong
	traces at Handan	early 4th cent. B.C.	Hebei
	traces at Xiadu	4th cent. B.C.	Hebei
Qin & Han (221 B.C.–A.D. 220)	traces at Xianyang	221–06 B.C.	Shânxi
	traces at Changan	206 B.C.–A.D. 9	Shânxi
	traces at Luoyang	A.D. 25–220	Henan
	Qin Shi huang di's mound	210 B.C.	Shânxi
	Liye pillar (que)	A.D. 28	Zidong, Sichuan
	Huangshengqing pillar (que)	A.D. 85	Pingyi, Feixian, Shandong
	Gaoyi pillar (que)	A.D. 209	Yaan, Sichuan
Three Kingdoms & Six Dynasties (221–589)	tombs of southern dynasties	5th–6th cent.	near Nanking, Jiangsu
	Dunhuang caves	after 353	Gansu
	Yungang caves	after 450	Shânxi
	Longmen caves	after 495	Henan
	Songye si pagoda	523	Song shan, Henan
	Simen ta of Shentong si	544	Licheng, Shandong
Sui (590–617) & Tang (618–907)	Anji qiao (bridge)	606–18	Zhaoxian, Hebei
	traces at Changan: Daming gong	634	Shânxi
	Dayan ta	701–4	Sian, Shânxi
	Xiaoyan ta	707	Sian, Shânxi
	main hall of Foguang si	857	Wutai shan, Shânxi
	Jingchuang of Foguang si	877	Wutai shan, Shânxi
Five Dynasties (907–959) & Northern Song (960–1126)	Wang Jian's tomb	918	Chengdu, Sichuan
	Heli ta of Qixia si	937–75	Nanking, Jiangsu
	Keifeng, Northern Song capital	960–1126	Henan
	Huqiu pagoda	961	Suzhou, Jiangsu
	Jingchuang of Lingyin si	969	Hangzhou, Zhejiang
	Longxing si	971	Zhengding, Hebei
	twin pagodas (Shuang ta)	984–7	Suzhou, Jiangsu
	Dacheng dian of Xianwen miao	10th cent.	Zhengsing, Hebei
	Ruigang si pagoda	10th–12th cent.	Suzhou, Jiangsu
	Tie ta of Youguo si	1049	Kaifeng, Henan
	Luoyang qiao	1053–9	Quanzhou, Fujian
	Xiangguo si	11th cent.	Kaifeng, Henan
	Chuzu an of Shaolin si	1125	Song shan, Henan
	Wenshu pavilion of Foguang si	1137	Wutai shan, Shânxi
	Beisi da ta	mid 11th cent.	Suzhou, Jiangsu

Dynasty	Monuments	Date	Location
Liao (907–1125) & Jin (1125–1234)	Peking: southern Liao capital	from 936	Hebei
	Dule si (Guanyin ge & Shanmen)	984	Jixian, Hebei
	Shijia pagoda of Fogong si	1056	Yingxian, Shanxi
	Shanhua si (Daxiong dian)	11th–12th cent.	Datong, Shanxi
	Peking: Jin capital	from 1125	Hebei
	Tianning si pagoda	early 12th cent.	Peking, Hebei
	Baima si pagoda	1175	Luoyang, Henan
	Lugou qiao (Marco Polo Bridge)	1189–1192	Peking, Hebei
Southern Song (1127–1279)	Hangzhou: Southern Song capital	1127–1279	Zhejiang
	Liuhe ta	from 1153	Hangzhou, Zhejiang
	Sanqing dian of Xuanmiao guan	1179	Suzhou, Jiangsu
	twin pagodas of Kaiyuan si	1228–50	Quanzhou, Fujian
Yuan (1280–1367)	Peking: Mongol capital	from 1264	Hebei
	Yongle gong	1247–1358	Ruicheng, Shanxi
	White Dagoba of Miaoying si	1271	Peking, Hebei
	Zushou si pagoda	Yuan & Ming	Balizhuang, Peking, Hel
Ming (1368–1643)	Nanking: Ming capital	1368–1409	Jiangsu
	Hong wu's tomb	late 14th cent.	Nanking, Jiangsu
	Great Wall (present state)	1368–1500	
	Peking: Ming capital	1409–1643	Hebei
	Drum Tower	early Ming	Sian, Shânxi
	Imperial Palace, Peking (Gugong)	begun 1406	Peking, Hebei
	Ming Tombs	15th–17th cent.	near Peking, Hebei
	Temple of Heaven	1420	Peking, Hebei
	Drum Tower	1420	Peking, Hebei
	Zhihua si	1443	Peking, Hebei
	Wuta si	1473	Peking, Hebei
	Temple of Confucius	early 16th cent.	Qufu, Shandong
	Biyun si dagoba	16th cent.	Peking, Hebei
	Wuliang dian of Kaiyuan si	1618	Suzhou, Jiangsu
Qing (1644–1911)	Peking: Qing capital	from 1644	Hebei
	Beihai white dagoba	1652	Peking, Hebei
	Dazhong si	1733	Peking, Hebei
	Clock Tower	1745	Peking, Hebei
	Huang si dagoba	1780	Peking, Hebei

ei

Bibliography

Balazs, E.
La Bureaucratie céleste. Paris, 1968

Bouillard, G. & Vaudescal
Les Sépultures impériales des Ming (Che-san-ling).
Bulletin de l'Ecole Française d'Extrême-Orient,
XX, 1920, 3, Hanoi

Boyd, A.
Chinese Architecture and Town Planning
(1500 B.C.–A.D. 1911). London, 1962

Bulling, A.
Buddhist Temples in the T'ang Period. Oriental Art,
1955, I, London

Kwang-chih Chang
The Archaeology of Ancient China. Yale University
Press, 1968 (revised & expanded edition)

Cheng Mingda
Zhongguo jianzhu gaishuo (short summary of Chinese
architecture) W.W.T.K.T.L. No. 3, 1958, Peking

Chuta Ito
Architectural Decoration in China. 5 Fol.,
Tohu Bunka Gakuin, Tokyo, 1941–43

Demiéville, P.
Che-yin Song Li Ming-tchong Ying tsao fa che.
Edition photolithographique de la méthode
d'architecture de Li Mingtchong des Song. 8 fasc. 1920
(Review in Bulletin de l'Ecole Française
d'Extrême-Orient, 1925, Hanoi)

Du Xianzhou
Yongle gong di jianzhu (The Architecture of the
Yongle gong). Wen Wu, 1963, No. 8, Peking

Ecke, G. & Demiéville, P.
The Twin Pagodas of Zayton. Harvard Yenching
Institute, Vol. II, Harvard University Press, 1935,
Cambridge, Mass.

Ecke, G.
Structural Features of the Stone-built T'ing Pagoda.
Monumenta Serica, 1935–1936, Peking

Ecke, G.
The Institute for Research in Chinese Architecture,
a short summary of the field work carried on from
spring 1932 to spring 1937. Monumenta Serica,
1936–1937, Peking

Gernet, J.
La Vie quotidienne en Chine à la Veille de l'Invasion
mongole, 1250–1276. Paris, 1959

Granet, Marcel
La Civilisation chinoise. Paris, 1948

Huizhou Mingdai zhuzhai (Ming period habitations
in Huizhou), Peking, 1957

Kelling, R.
Das chinesische Wohnhaus. Tokyo, 1935

Liu Dunzhen
Zhongguo zhuzhai gaishuo (short report on habitation
in China). Peking, 1957

Qi Yingtao
Zhongguo gudai jianzhu niandai di jianding
(Dating in ancient chinese architecture). Wen Wu,
N. 4–5, 1965, Peking

Segalen, V., de Voisins, G., Lartigue, J.
L'Art funéraire à l'époque Han – mission archéologique
en Chine (1914). Paris, 1935

Sickman, L. & Soper, A.
The Art and Architecture of China. London, 1956

Sirén, O.
The Walls and Gates of Peking. London, 1924

Sirén, O.
Gardens of China. New York, 1949

Sirén, O.
Les Palais impériaux de Péking. 3 vol., Van Oest,
Paris & Bruxelles, 1926

Sirén, O.
Tch'ang-ngan au temps des Souei et des T'ang. Revue
des Arts Asiatiques, No. 1–2, Paris, 1927

Sirén, O.
Histoire des Arts anciens en Chine. Vol. IV:
architecture. Van Oest, Paris & Bruxelles, 1930

Soper, Alexander C.
The Evolution of Buddhist Architecture in Japan.
London, 1942

Stein, Rolf A.
Jardin en miniature d'Extrême-Orient. Bulletin de
l'Ecole Française d'Extrême-Orient, Hanoi, 1942

Stein, Rolf A.
L'Habitat, le Monde et le Corps humain en
Extrême-Orient et en Haute-Asie. Journal Asiatique,
fasc. 1, Paris, 1957

Stein, Rolf A.
Architecture et Pensée religieuse en Extrême-Orient.
Arts Asiatiques t. IV, fasc. 3, Paris, 1957

Tang Changan Daming gong
(The Daming Palace of Changan of the Tang).
Peking, 1959

Tang Huancheng
Zhongguo gudai qiaoliang (Ancient Chinese Bridges).
Peking, 1957

Willetts, W.
Chinese Art. Vol. II. London, 1958

Wright, Arthur F.
Symbolism and Function. Reflections on Changan and
other great cities. The Journal of Asian Studies,
Vol. XXIV, No. 4, August 1965, Ann Arbor, Mich.

Yetts, Percival W.
A Chinese Treatise on Architecture. Bulletin of the
School of Oriental Studies, Vol. IV, Part III, London,
1927

Zhongguo yingzao xue shi hui kan. Bulletin of the
Society for Research in Chinese Architecture, Vol. IV,
No. 3–4, June 1934, Peiping

Zhongguo jianzhu jianshi, I: Zhongguo gudai jianshu
jianshi. A Short History of Chinese Architecture, I:
Ancient Architecture, Peking, 1962

Photographs by the Courtesy of:

Arthaud Claude, Paris: pp. 21, 68, 69, 110, 124

Burri René, Zurich (Magnum): pp. 18, 61, 66, 67, 81, 108, 109, 118, 119

Camera Press, London (China Photo-Service): pp. 62–63, 117, 130

Cartier-Bresson Henri, Paris (Magnum): p. 26

Graf zu Castell, Munich: pp. 19, 20, 30, 64, 78, 79, 122, 153

Charbonnier J. Ph., Paris (Réalités): pp. 36, 73, 125, 128, 129

Darbois Dominique, Paris: pp. 107, 158b

Fonds Deonna, Geneva: p. 31

Etienne Gilbert, Geneva: p. 84

Gampert Photo, Montreal: p. 83

Gigon Fernand, Geneva: couverture et pp. 29, 65, 74, 158a

Hoppenot Hélène, Paris: pp. 76, 159, 160

Koch Paolo, Zurich: pp. 24, 25, 27, 32, 82, 113, 115, 123, 127, 155, 161, 163, 167c, in-text: pp. 8 left, 172 left

Koch Paolo, Zurich (Len Sirman Press): pp. 22–23, 28, 35a, 35b, 70, 71, 75, 77, 80, 114a, 114b, 120, 126, 156, 157, 164, 165, 167b, 168

Mazery Photo, Paris: p. 34

Pirazzoli-t'Serstevens Michèle, Paris: pp. 116, 154, 162, 166, 167a

Riboud Marc, Paris (Magnum): pp. 72, 111, 121

Schulthess Emile, Zurich: p. 17

S.E.C.A.S. Photo, Paris: p. 33

Roger-Viollet, Paris: p. 112

191

Printed in Switzerland

Dynasty	Monuments	Date	Location
Liao (907–1125) & Jin (1125–1234)	Peking: southern Liao capital	from 936	Hebei
	Dule si (Guanyin ge & Shanmen)	984	Jixian, Hebei
	Shijia pagoda of Fogong si	1056	Yingxian, Shanxi
	Shanhua si (Daxiong dian)	11th–12th cent.	Datong, Shanxi
	Peking: Jin capital	from 1125	Hebei
	Tianning si pagoda	early 12th cent.	Peking, Hebei
	Baima si pagoda	1175	Luoyang, Henan
	Lugou qiao (Marco Polo Bridge)	1189–1192	Peking, Hebei
Southern Song (1127–1279)	Hangzhou: Southern Song capital	1127–1279	Zhejiang
	Liuhe ta	from 1153	Hangzhou, Zhejiang
	Sanqing dian of Xuanmiao guan	1179	Suzhou, Jiangsu
	twin pagodas of Kaiyuan si	1228–50	Quanzhou, Fujian
Yuan (1280–1367)	Peking: Mongol capital	from 1264	Hebei
	Yongle gong	1247–1358	Ruicheng, Shanxi
	White Dagoba of Miaoying si	1271	Peking, Hebei
	Zushou si pagoda	Yuan & Ming	Balizhuang, Peking, Hei
Ming (1368–1643)	Nanking: Ming capital	1368–1409	Jiangsu
	Hong wu's tomb	late 14th cent.	Nanking, Jiangsu
	Great Wall (present state)	1368–1500	
	Peking: Ming capital	1409–1643	Hebei
	Drum Tower	early Ming	Sian, Shânxi
	Imperial Palace, Peking (Gugong)	begun 1406	Peking, Hebei
	Ming Tombs	15th–17th cent.	near Peking, Hebei
	Temple of Heaven	1420	Peking, Hebei
	Drum Tower	1420	Peking, Hebei
	Zhihua si	1443	Peking, Hebei
	Wuta si	1473	Peking, Hebei
	Temple of Confucius	early 16th cent.	Qufu, Shandong
	Biyun si dagoba	16th cent.	Peking, Hebei
	Wuliang dian of Kaiyuan si	1618	Suzhou, Jiangsu
Qing (1644–1911)	Peking: Qing capital	from 1644	Hebei
	Beihai white dagoba	1652	Peking, Hebei
	Dazhong si	1733	Peking, Hebei
	Clock Tower	1745	Peking, Hebei
	Huang si dagoba	1780	Peking, Hebei

ei

Printed in Switzerland